Worlds to Explore

Brownie and Junior Leaders' Guide

Girl Scouts of the U.S.A.
830 Third Avenue
New York, N.Y. 10022

Inquiries related to *Worlds to Explore: Brownie and Junior Leaders' Guide* should be addressed to
the Program Department,
Girl Scouts of the U.S.A.,
830 Third Avenue, New York, N.Y. 10022.

Girl Scouts of the U.S.A.

Dr. Gloria D. Scott, President

Frances R. Hesselbein, National Executive Director

Authors/Contributors

Patricia Connally

Judy Cook

Nancy Garfield

Carol Green

Mabel Hammersmith

Hillary Hemans

Dorothy Kennedy

Ely List

Elizabeth Munz

Corinne Murphy

Carolyn Wool

Consultant

Joan McEniry

Designer

Edward Lessing

Handbook page references in this book relate to *Worlds to Explore: Handbook for Brownie and Junior Girl Scouts*.

Contents

To Leaders, With Love

Girl Scout leadership is always challenging, often difficult, and rarely without surprises. Whether you've just begun, or have had years of leadership experience, you have probably discovered this for yourself; such facts do not remain hidden for long!

Much that you learn about being an effective leader will emerge from your own direct experience, not from books. But in Girl Scouting, "learning for yourself" has never meant starting from scratch, as if no one had ever done this sort of thing before. For you, as for the girls, tackling new things need not imply facing each problem alone or inventing answers to your own questions.

New or experienced, you naturally seek help and guidance from others who, like you, care about girls—and who, out of that caring, have shaped the practical knowledge and skills that help make Girl Scout leadership joyous and worthwhile.

Many such people have helped to write this book. It is written to you, with love, to help you enjoy meeting the challenge you have accepted: the challenge of walking a while with girls through wondrous, hectic, sometimes frightening years of growing up. With this challenge comes the privilege of helping girls find in themselves the very best that they can be.

Here is basic information about Girl Scouting and the Girl Scout program, to be used along with the girls' own book, *Worlds to Explore: Handbook for Brownie and Junior Girl Scouts.* Here, also, are tips and how-to's to help you handle difficulties as they arise and deal creatively with the surprises of Girl Scout leadership.

Without you, the Girl Scout program could not exist. It is your enthusiasm that makes the spirit of Girl Scouting come alive for girls. It is your understanding and skill that offer them opportunities to grow through the fun and friendship of a troop. It is your wisdom, caring, and love that move the goals and ideals of Girl Scouting from wish to reality for girls.

For girls reaching out to touch, understand, and affect their world, you are a friend, guide, and partner. The power of this partnership can give you, as well as the girls you serve, a lifelong zest for living, learning, and growing.

About Girl Scouting

The Promise and Law:
The Foundation of
Girl Scouting

Girl Scouting in the United States is part of a worldwide movement with members in more than 90 nations, banded together through the World Association of Girl Guides and Girl Scouts.

The spiritual force of the movement and the ethical code accepted by all of its members are expressed in the Promise and Law. Although there are some variations in wording from one country to another, the principles are always the same.

Everyone who joins Girl Scouting in the United States makes the Promise as follows:

On my honor, I will try

To serve God, my country and mankind,

And to live by the Girl Scout Law.

The Law we promise to live by is:

I will do my best:

-to be honest

-to be fair

-to help where I am needed

-to be cheerful

-to be friendly and considerate

-to be a sister to every Girl Scout

-to respect authority

-to use resources wisely

-to protect and improve the world around me

-to show respect for myself and others through my words and actions.

The Girl Scout program is built on the foundation of this ethical code. Its guiding principles are:

-belief in God

-service

-responsible citizenship

-high ideals of character and conduct

-appreciation of the worth of all people.

Girl Scout Ways of Work

As a natural part of her activities in Girl Scouting, each girl can find personal meaning in the Promise and Law. She can discover for herself the rewards as well as the difficulties of living by one's beliefs. She can see a code of ethics as a part of everyday actions and relationships, not as a set of arbitrary rules.

For girls and adults, "I will try" and "I will do my best" are reminders that the goal is not perfection; that for each individual, living up to ideals calls for her own finest efforts.

You will find more about the Promise and Law on pages 7-11 of the handbook and pages 30-31 of this leaders' guide.

Girl Scouting operates on the principle that girls grow, learn, and have fun by making decisions, doing, and discovering for themselves. The Girl Scout program is carried out through ways of work that support the aim of helping each girl develop to her fullest potential through group experience.

Here are some of the key features of these ways of work. Combined with the Girl Scout Promise and Law, uniforms, slogan and motto, and the voluntary nature of the Girl Scout movement, they help to create the unique character of Girl Scouting.

Small Groups: Girls work in troops or smaller units within the troop so that they will have opportunities to be active participants—to speak, be heard, influence decisions, try new things for themselves, and develop leadership skills.

Self-Government: Girls learn to govern themselves in a democratic way, selecting their own girl leaders, delegating authority, accepting responsibility for plans and action. Troop activities come from the girls' ideas, and the entire group is involved in planning and decision-making.

Girl-Adult Partnership: Girls and their adult leaders work together in close partnership based on shared interests. Leaders support girls in their efforts to become responsible and self-reliant individuals, providing friendship, advice, encouragement, and resources. Each partner's responsibilities are agreed upon by girls and adults; each partner does her share to make the troop fun and productive for everyone.

These ways of work develop through practice, with girls taking on a greater part of the responsibility as they are able. At first, young girls may rely heavily on their adult partners, but with sensitive guidance, girls of any age can become increasingly independent. The roles and responsibilities of girls and adults will change as the partnership progresses.

Key Aspects of Girl Scouting Fit Together to Form the Design for Girl Scout Program

8

The Girl Scout Promise and Law:
The Foundation of Girl Scouting
See page 7.

The Four Program Emphases:
Our Goals for Girls
See page 9.

Five Worlds of Interest:
Activity Areas
See page 10.

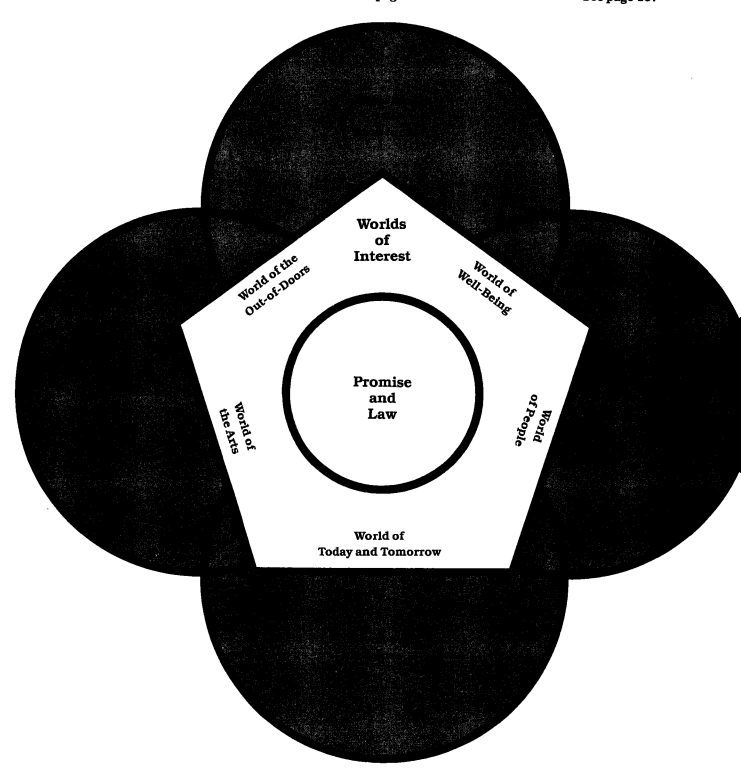

Worlds
of
Interest

World of the
Out-of-Doors

World of
Well-Being

World of
the Arts

Promise
and
Law

World
of People

World of
Today and Tomorrow

You'll find information about Girl Scout ways of work throughout this book, particularly in the second and third chapters. The national Program Standards on pages 87-91 offer specific guidelines for high quality program. (Don't forget to find out about your own council's standards, too.)

Forms of self-government for troops are explained in *Worlds to Explore: Handbook for Brownie and Junior Girl Scouts* under the headings "Becoming a Brownie" and "Troop Government."

The Four Program Emphases:
Our Goals for Girls

The four Program Emphases sum up the ways in which we hope each individual will grow through her Girl Scout experiences. In Girl Scout program, the goal for everything we do is the realization for each girl of these kinds of growth.

Deepening awareness of self as a unique person of worth.

Help the girl to develop feelings of being liked and needed □ to see herself as increasingly able, competent, and responsible □ to accept herself and see her own potential □ to build and maintain her own individuality □ to keep open to new experiences, feelings, and challenges.

Relating to others with increasing skill, maturity, and satisfaction.

Help her develop sensitivity and respect for the needs, feelings, and contributions of others □ a sense of oneness with others □ an ability to build friendships and working relationships.

Developing values to give meaning and direction to her life.

Help her to be aware of, and act in accordance with, her own values □ to make decisions in the light of consequences and what is important to her and others □ to

develop confidence and sensitivity that will allow her to appreciate diverse beliefs □ to reexamine her ideals as she grows and changes.

Contributing to the betterment of her society through use of her own talents and in cooperative effort with others.

Help her to develop concern for her community, its people and needs □ to see how the quality of community life affects her own life and the whole of society □ to work with others for the benefit of all.

Growth in each of these four interrelated areas is supported by a troop atmosphere of openness, freedom, and trust, and by program activities that encourage each girl to:

Discover ways to express herself and communicate with others.

Understand and appreciate other people and other cultures.

Make choices from among real alternatives.

Recognize and build on her own talents and interests.

Grapple with and solve problems.

Help develop standards for her own behavior and accomplishment.

Take responsibility for her actions.

Use knowledge and skills in challenging situations.

Be teacher and learner, giver and receiver.

Make mistakes without the stigma of failure.

Explore the many roles and unlimited potential of women.

Work cooperatively with others toward common goals.

Have fun and build friendships.

Test her values in action.

Become an active partner in her community.

Five Worlds of Interest: Activity Areas

"Doing things" and "having fun" are high on the list of what girls look for in Girl Scouting. Through activities that girls enjoy, the concepts of the Promise and Law and the four Program Emphases come alive for them. Girl Scouting offers a variety of experiences and adventures that increase the girls' understanding of the community, each other, and themselves.

To provide this variety, and to help girls select from virtually endless possibilities, the Girl Scout program groups activities into five broad interest areas:

The World of Well-Being includes activities that focus on physical and emotional health: nutrition and exercise □ interpersonal relationships □ the home □ safety □ work and leisure □ consumer awareness.

The World of People includes activities that focus on developing awareness of the various cultures in our society and around the world, and on building pride in one's heritage while appreciating and respecting that of others.

The World of Today and Tomorrow includes activities that focus on discovering the how and why of things □ exploring and experimenting with many technologies that touch daily life □ dealing with change □ looking to future events, roles, and responsibilities.

The World of the Arts includes activities that focus on involvement in the whole range of arts—visual, performing, literary □ enjoying and expressing one's self through various art forms □ appreciating the artistic talents and contributions of others.

The World of the Out-Of-Doors includes activities that focus on enjoyment and appreciation of the out-of-doors □ living in and caring for our natural environment □ understanding and respecting the interdependence of all living things.

The activity suggestions in these Worlds are not meant to reflect all of a girl's actual world. Rather, they help girls to frame a portion of their world and make it more understandable, so that action in the world at large—and impact on it—can be seen as possible. Each of the Worlds offers stepping-stones to deeper explorations as girls grow.

The specific activities girls select will be determined by their personal needs and interests. Also, as no two groups are exactly alike, there is much room for troop and individual choice and style. The growth opportunities stressed in the four Program Emphases can permeate all activities and all Worlds of interest; so a leader can feel free to let the girls choose what they want to do.

You help girls with the ins and outs of choosing, planning, solving problems, and seeing a project through. It is through these processes, as well as in the content of the activity itself, that the girls learn.

The girls' handbook contains basic information and many activity ideas and how-to's for each of the five Worlds of interest.

Chapter 4 of this leaders' guide describes the aims and focus of each World and the kinds of things girls can learn through their explorations. It also provides additional ideas for activities in each World.

Chapter 2 of this book (about being a leader), and Chapter 3 (particularly the sections about Brownie and Junior Girl Scouting) offer guidelines for helping girls choose, plan, carry out, and evaluate activities.

At whatever age a girl joins Girl Scouting, she can enjoy program activities designed to appeal to her interests and respond to her needs.

The Girl Scout Promise and Law and the four Program Emphases permeate activities in five Worlds of interest at every age level.

Girls can enter and progress in Girl Scouting at any one of four age levels.

	Brownie Girl Scouts	Junior Girl Scouts	Cadette Girl Scouts	Senior Girl Scouts
Age or Grade	6-8 years old or in first, second, or third grade	9-11 years old or in fourth, fifth, or sixth grade	12-14 years old* or in seventh, eighth, or ninth grade	14-17 years old* or in ninth, tenth, eleventh, or twelfth grade
Form of Government	Brownie Ring with committees	Patrol system, steering committee, or town meeting	Patrol system, steering committee, or town meeting	Patrol system, steering committee, or other form developed by troop
Activities and Opportunities Beyond the Troop	Community visits, events, and service Intertroop activities Council activities	Community visits, events, and service Intertroop activities Council activities National Center visits	Community visits, events, and service Intertroop activities Council activities Intercouncil activities National Center visits Regional/national events	Community visits, events, and service Intertroop activities Council activities Intercouncil activities National Center visits Regional/national events International events
Recognitions That Help Focus Activities	Brownie B Patches Bridge to Juniors Patch	Junior Badges Junior Aide Patch Sign of the Arrow Sign of the Star	Cadette Badges Cadette Challenges First Class	Aide Bars LIT (Leader in Training) CIT (Counselor in Training)

*A girl who is 14 years old or in the ninth grade may choose to be either a Cadette or a Senior.

Membership and Registration

Membership in the Girl Scout movement in the U.S.A. entitles girls and adults to participate in Girl Scout troop activities and other Girl Scout-sponsored events, to wear the appropriate uniform and insignia, and to be covered by Girl Scout accident insurance. In addition, adult members receive the *Girl Scout Leader,* the official GSUSA magazine, and are entitled to receive training, consultation, and ongoing assistance to do their jobs.

Through the membership of Girl Scouts of the U.S.A. in the World Association of Girl Guides and Girl Scouts, all Girl Scouts are entitled to wear the World Association pin. Older girls and adults may have opportunities to participate in international events sponsored by the World Association or by member countries.

Active membership as a Girl Scout is granted to any girl who:

o has made the Girl Scout Promise and accepted the Girl Scout Law;

o is a participating member in the Girl Scout program;

o has paid annual membership dues of two dollars;

o meets applicable membership standards.

Active membership as a Girl Scout adult is granted to any person who:

o accepts the principles and beliefs as stated in the Preamble of the Constitution;

o has paid annual membership dues of two dollars;

o is working in the organization in a defined adult capacity;

o meets applicable membership standard.

Applicable membership standards for girls are the age-or-grade descriptions of each age level given at the top of the chart on page 11 of this book. The applicable membership standard for adults, both women and men, is that they must be at least 18 years old.

The Promise and Law are given on page 7 of this book. The Preamble of the Constitution of Girl Scouts of the U.S.A. begins with the Promise and Law and continues as follows:

Beliefs and Principles
We, the members of Girl Scouts of the United States of America, united by a belief in God and by acceptance of the Girl Scout Promise and Law,

And inspired by the aims of the Founder of the Scout movement, Lord Baden-Powell, and of the Founder of the Girl Scout movement in the United States, Juliette Low,

Do dedicate ourselves to the purpose of inspiring girls with the highest ideals of character, conduct, patriotism, and service that they may become happy and resourceful citizens.

We believe that the motivating force in Girl Scouting is a spiritual one.

We affirm that the Girl Scout movement shall ever be open to all girls and adults who accept the Girl Scout Promise and Law.

We maintain that the strength of the Girl Scout movement rests in the voluntary leadership of its adult members, in the cooperation and support of the community, and in the affiliation with Girl Guide and Girl Scout movements of other countries through the World Association of Girl Guides and Girl Scouts.

We declare that the democratic way of life and the democratic process shall guide all our activities.

We hold that ultimate responsibility for the Girl Scout movement rests with volunteers.

National Membership Registration

As a leader, you are responsible for registering all girl and adult members of your troop and collecting national membership dues each year. Your Girl Scout council will supply registration forms and instructions for completing them. The council will also designate a month for the troop's annual reregistration.

If additional members join during the year, be sure to register them promptly so that they can receive the full benefits of Girl Scout membership, including the very important activity accident insurance. Those who join more than six months after the troop's regular registration month will pay partial dues. Others will pay a full year's dues.

National registration procedures are described on pages 12 and 13 of your *Leader's Digest of Blue Book of Basic Documents.*

When they pay annual membership dues, girls might want to know what the money is used for. Here are some of the things that the national organization does for girls:

gathers ideas for what girls want to do in Girl Scouting

puts these ideas together in a program for all girls

publishes books that explain the Girl Scout program and supply information girls and leaders need (the most important are handbooks and leaders' guides)

supplies uniforms, pins, badges, and all of the other equipment shown in the Girl Scout catalog

publishes two magazines for girls, *Daisy* and *American Girl,* and the *Girl Scout Leader* magazine for the adult membership.

National services of special importance to you as a leader are described on page 29 of this leaders' guide.

About Being a Brownie or Junior Girl Scout Leader

What Girls Want and Need

Some things don't change. Back in 1943, you would have read these words in *Leadership of Girl Scout Troops:*

> A girl growing up these days needs a variety of things. She needs friends of her own age and the feeling that they like and accept her for what she is. She wants to feel important and useful as an individual by knowing how to do some things well. She wants information on all sorts of subjects—some of which she does not get in school or at home. She wants plenty of activity that is lively, fun, adventurous. ...She wants an older, understanding friend to whom she can talk. The trust and affection of older people, both within and without her family circle, are very important to her—although often one would never suspect it. ... Girls need to see the problems of ethics, group living, and democracy worked out in a girl-sized setting they can understand. A community that cares for its own future will see that girls have this opportunity.

It's still true, all of it.

What Is Leadership?

There is no easy definition of leadership, for leadership involves being as well as doing. Individual styles of leadership may be quite different yet equally effective. It is possible, however, to list some things that every leader does.

In any group, the leader is one who

o supplies a sense of direction

o moves the group toward agreement on shared goals

o sees that each member's part in reaching goals is understood

o keeps an eye on individual progress and on relationships between individuals

o knows and interprets rules that apply to the group

o is held accountable for the group.

In a Girl Scout troop, leadership takes on special meaning. It means feeling a sense of kinship with girls, understanding and caring for them, wanting to help toward their growth and development. It means listening, teaching, advising, supporting, learning, and occasionally picking up the pieces. It means sharing a relationship with girls that is different from their relationships with other adults in their lives.

What Girls Expect from Their Leaders

Just as you may expect certain things of girls, they may expect you, as their leader, to show certain qualities and act in certain ways. You are a model for them; usually, unspoken in their expectations is the desire to be and act like you. Here are some of the things girls look for in their adult leaders.

Recognition and Acceptance. Girls look up to their leaders. They need to know that you consider each of them as an important person. They can survive a poor meeting place or an activity that flops. But they cannot long endure being ignored or rejected.

Recognize acts of trying as well as instances of clear success. Emphasize the positive qualities that make each girl worthy and unique. Be generous with praise and stingy with rebuke. *Help girls find ways to show acceptance and support for one another.*

Fairness. Girls are sensitive to injustice. They forgive mistakes if they are sure that you try to be fair. They look for fairness in the ways responsibilities are shared, in the handling of disagreements, in responses to performance and accomplishment.

Consult girls as to what they think is fair before decisions are made. Explain your reasoning and show why you did something. Be willing to apologize if it is needed. Try to see that the chances for feeling important, as well as the responsibilities, are equally divided. *Help girls explore and decide for themselves the fair ways of solving problems, carrying out activities, and looking at behavior and accomplishment.*

Trust. Girls need your belief in them and your support when they try new things. They must be sure that you will not betray a confidence.

Show girls you trust them to think for themselves and use their own judgment. Help them make the important decisions in the troop. Help them correct their own mistakes. *Help girls give and show trust toward one another. Help them see how trust can be built, lost, strengthened.*

Open Communication. Girls want someone who will listen seriously to what they think and feel and want to do. They like someone they can talk to about important things, including some that might not seem important to adults.

Listen to girls. Respond with both words and action. Speak your mind openly when you are happy or concerned about something, and encourage girls to do this, too. Leave the door open for girls to seek advice, share ideas and feelings, propose plans or improvements. *Help girls see how open communication can result in action, discovery, better understanding of self and others, a more comfortable climate for fun and accomplishment.*

If you are in doubt about expectations—yours or the girls'—it will repay you a hundredfold to discuss this with them directly.

Remember that the Promise and Law are a guide to the things that all Girl Scouts, girl or adult, should be able to expect from one another. All of us promise that we will try to live up to these high ideals. As you and the girls learn to recognize acts of trying in one another, understanding grows and the give-and-take becomes easier.

Some Skills for Relating Positively to Girls

To meet the expectations girls often have of their leader, and to build comfortable working relationships with girls, here are some basic skills that a leader can use:

Listening and Responding—A First Step to Trust: Many adults tend to talk *at* children. They don't give the child a chance to express herself. Or, when they listen, they may not make a special effort to really hear what a child is saying.

Encourage girls to tell you more; ask questions to draw out what they want to say:

"I know that something has upset you. Can (or will) you tell me about it?"

"I'd like to get your ideas (or opinions) about _____."

"Tell me! I'm excited to hear about it."

"That does sound serious (exciting, like fun, scary, etc.). Please tell me more."

Support girls in their effort to communicate:

"A lot of us feel that way sometimes, Judy."

"I'm so glad you told me, Maria."

"Wow! I like that idea (approach, solution)."

"Thank you, that is a very helpful thought."

Respond with both words and actions. Let the girls know that you really heard them and really do think about what they say:

"I'm very sorry, I didn't realize you felt that way. Would it help if I _____?" (Suggest a specific solution.)

"You're right. Let's talk about it right now and see what we can *do* about it."

"Debbie (hug), you've made me very happy by saying that."

"I think I understand better now. I'll need a little time to think about this. (Let me think about it this evening—or between now and [give time].)"

Reading and Using Body Language. People can communicate with words—and also with their body movements. They can say things by facial expression (frowning, smiling), by how close or far they sit from each other, by touching someone.

A hug, an arm around a shoulder, a smile or nod of approval or support can often mean a great deal to a girl who needs reassurance. Girls are seeking positive feelings from you. And they are friends who can help you when *you* need reassurance.

Watch for unspoken signs of disapproval in yourself: pointing or shaking a finger, raising your eyebrows, closing your eyes, pushing a girl away, frowning, clenching your fists, sighing. If there is a reason you are acting in a certain way (a severe headache, a bill that came in today's mail), let the girls know that other things, and not they, are worrying you.

Look for the ways girls express themselves through actions. Laughing, jumping up and down, buzzing around you, hand-holding, standing close to you, touching your jewelry can all be positive signs. But watch out for signs of unhappiness or boredom. Yawning, clock-watching, crying, back turning, consistently coming late, hitting and pushing, breaking things, constant fidgeting can tell you that something is wrong, or that a change of pace or activity may be needed.

Giving and Receiving Praise. We all appreciate sincere praise that recognizes our efforts and accomplishments.

Tell a girl when her actions make you feel pleased, happy, proud.

Praise without condescending—or overwhelming.

Watch out for put-down expressions ("That's a good little girl." "Yes, darling, that's very cute.").

Try to translate "marvelous," "perfect," "excellent," "good" into more specific terms. (Exactly what was it about her actions that made them worthy of admiration?) Vague or over-enthusiastic praise can leave a girl wondering what she actually did to get such results. Angel wings pinned on one moment can easily be tripped over in the next. They can immobilize a girl completely if she doesn't feel worthy or is afraid to take a chance on "breaking the spell."

Accept praise with a "thank you" whenever praise is given. Be willing to settle for "You're swell!" from some girls, "You're not bad" from others, and a lot in between. It may be awkward for some girls to express appreciation in words. This kind of give-and-take grows with time, and with the realization of what is appropriate.

How Girls Develop And How You Can Help

Many Dimensions of Growth

Children develop in many different ways: physically □ intellectually □ socially □ emotionally □ morally.

Physically. Children first learn by using their senses. They discover the world around them by touching, smelling, tasting, hearing, and seeing. As they grow, they increase motor skills. As they become more coordinated, they learn additional skills. Toward the end of Juniors, some girls may have reached puberty. All of these complex changes in muscles, organs, and body frame affect the interests girls have, the skills they can master, and their own sense of ability to cope with the physical demands of daily living.

Intellectually. As children develop, their mental structure becomes more complex. They put ideas together into patterns, building concepts out of concrete experiences. They increase their ability to use ideas, solve problems, plan, imagine, and project into the future. Each new or related experience with people, things, and ideas adds to a child's growing fund of reliable information.

Socially. Children move from concern only with self toward greater interest in and understanding of others. They become increasingly independent of adults and become more involved in relationships with other children. They start thinking about how other people will react to what they do. The impact of their own culture and society affects the way they see their world and their present and future roles in it.

Emotionally. Young children express their feelings freely and physically. As they grow, they learn to become more restrained in showing their emotions. But, as they do, the feelings often become stronger and longer lasting. They start considering the feelings of others and learn to channel emotional energy into a variety of ways of self-expression and self-protection.

Morally. The ethical sense evolves gradually from dependence on yes-no absolutes of behavior (to win adult approval or avoid punishment) toward an internal sense of right and wrong. Along with the ability to think more objectively, children begin to see rules and expectations as making sense in their own right. Their zigzag path from self-interest to social responsibility reflects a struggle between holding on to their newly emerging self and subordinating their own desires to the well-being of the whole. The process of moral development is similar for most children, regardless of the specific values they develop.

You can observe many of these kinds of growth in each girl as you watch, listen, and get to know her as an individual. As growth takes place in one or more of these areas, you might see outward evidence of change in such things as:

drawings □ vocabulary □ choice of games □ independence □ relationships with others □ movements □ sense of time □ conversations □ problem solving.

Each child progresses at different rates and in different ways. Some move rapidly in one area of development and slowly in another.

Some Things You Can Do to Enhance Each Girl's Development

View each girl as an individual. Accept her at her own level of development. This will help her to trust herself and to move ahead confidently at her own rate.

Avoid activities that call for all girls to do the same thing in the same way and to produce the same results.

Help girls vary games and other troop activities so that each girl has some opportunities to feel successful, whatever her level of development.

Encourage girls to assist *each other* with activities, plans, and tasks. A girl who has recently mastered a skill or a way of doing things may be more sensitive to another's needs, and be better able to offer practical help to another girl, than an adult. Pair or group girls in different ways (all same age, mixed ages, mixed abilities) so that they can support and supplement each other's abilities and efforts.

Encourage girls to do and experience things for themselves—to touch, listen, smell, and see, to test and strengthen their competencies by trying out new skills. And remember, things that may be "old hat" to you are bright and new to girls.

Help with new words and concepts as they come up, guiding girls to define these *from their own experiences,* not from the dictionary. (How does it look or feel? What is it used for? Where have you seen, tried, or heard of it? Who has ever felt or thought that way, or had that kind of experience?)

Avoid the temptation to rush things, to push girls quickly into next levels of development. Give them the opportunity to live freely at every stage of growth. Help girls benefit from *play;* it's an important part of their growing up.

Girls *like* to play. For most of them, it's something they do well. By six, they've had a lot of practice! Some rules of play have been passed along from child to child for generations without benefit of adult instruction in the process.

Through play, girls get acquainted with their world and test competence and relationships in their own terms. They use their senses, mind, and body, try out new skills, and learn to cope with conflict. In play, they combine fantasy and reality in ways that can strengthen creativity and imagination.

In the troop, girls might make clear distinctions between "work" and "play" activities (a game is "play"; planning is "work"). In doing this, they may be assigning a more grown-up importance to doing certain kinds of things. They need this sense of growth. But they may merely be reflecting adult attitudes toward these things. If no sharp work-play distinction is made by the leader, girls can see *all sorts of things* as fun to learn and do; that is, as a natural extension of play.

What A Leader Does

Just as there is no one definition of leadership, there can be no one formula that says how a leader goes about being a leader. Girl Scout leaders are not carbon copies of each other in action any more than they are in background, talent, or personality. Each brings to her role a storehouse of knowledge, skill, and experience that puts an individual stamp on her leadership efforts. But all share certain functions and responsibilities that make them distinctly Girl Scout leaders, operating within the Girl Scout program and using mutually-agreed-upon ways of work.

Building an atmosphere for growth: More important than the specific activities in a troop is the kind of atmosphere in which activities take place. As a leader, you work with girls to create and maintain a positive atmosphere for growth in which:

people, rather than things, are of prime importance.

individual differences are sought out, accepted, and respected as potentially enriching for all.

sincere trust, admiration, and understanding exist within the group.

questioning and wondering are encouraged and guided.

mistakes, as well as successes, have value for learning.

beliefs, ideas, concerns, and feelings may be expressed without fear.

creativity and self-help are encouraged and supported.

there is freedom from excessive competition.

acts of reaching out to others are encouraged.

there is freedom to weigh alternatives, make choices, and test the consequences of choice in action.

individuals are helped to try out various roles within the group.

there is freedom to talk about things in society as they really are.

there is encouragement to be aware of and protect the rights of all people.

there is support to live according to one's own ideals, and to examine and reexamine beliefs and convictions.

You help create an atmosphere of adventure and fun by:

having a sense of humor... or developing one.

relaxing and enjoying the girls. Don't be afraid to show you like them and like being with them.

allowing girls to enjoy themselves and what they are doing. Many serious things can be done in fun ways.

surprising them with a new thought, song, idea, game, visitor, or celebration.

encouraging inventive thinking, creativity, new problem-solving approaches.

allowing for spontaneity.

thinking big, going to new places, meeting new friends, inviting others to join the fun.

Being a Partner with Girls

Enjoying the experience of Girl Scouting is something that you and girls do together. As troop leader, you contribute adult knowledge and skills. You also recognize that each girl—whether she is a beginning Brownie or a Junior ready to bridge into Cadettes—has capabilities of her own and can make a contribution.

You and the girls share responsibility for making the troop run well. You grow with them through the process of trying, succeeding, sometimes failing, and learning from mistakes.

As an adult, you have certain special responsibilities in the partnership. Use the checklist below to discover how many of them you know about or are doing, which ones are especially rewarding for you, which ones you need help with.

Generating ideas and choosing activities:

☐ You encourage girls to express their ideas and interests.

☐ You suggest ideas for adventuresome things to do.

☐ You take part in sorting out ideas and combining them into possible projects and activities.

☐ You help girls to choose from among the many possible activities.

Planning activities:

☐ You help girls plan interesting, enjoyable ways to do the things they have chosen.

☐ You make specific suggestions.

☐ You give practical advice on budget, time, equipment, space, resources.

☐ You and the girls decide together who will do what parts of the plan.

Carrying out activities:

☐ You show girls how to do new things, or learn new things along with them.

☐ You give guidance in handling difficulties that arise while activities are in progress.

☐ You watch out for safety.

☐ You remind girls of their plan, if necessary, and help them to recognize the results of their ideas.

Evaluating activities:

☐ You congratulate girls on successes and help them face and examine things that went wrong.

☐ You point out ways that an experience can be useful in future adventures.

☐ You help girls to recognize what they have learned and to use it in a variety of ways, for themselves and others.

For more about your role in choosing, planning, carrying out, and evaluating troop activities, see pages 18-20 in this leaders' guide. The actual process will depend to a large extent on the form of self-government in the troop.

Troop government:

☐ You explain the Brownie Ring and committees or the three forms of troop government from which Juniors may choose, as described in the girls' handbook.

☐ You help girls set up a workable form of troop government.

☐ You provide support, advice, and know-how without taking over.

☐ You help girls to develop a feel for representative self-government, so that they can use the process successfully in planning, solving problems, and making important decisions.

☐ You make sure that girls have opportunities to try out various roles and responsibilities within the group.

☐ You give guidance and advice to troop officers.

☐ You are in charge of financial management, as you help girls to learn about budgeting, collecting dues, and keeping money records.

Basic information on the operation of Junior troop government is on pages 71-76 in the handbook. You will find more about troop government and budgeting for Brownies on pages 35-36 of this leaders' guide; for Juniors on pages 38-39.

Activities beyond the troop:

☐ You tell girls about and help them prepare for neighborhood and council events such as camping, play days, rallies, and celebrations.

☐ You help girls plan and enjoy intertroop activities with sister Girl Scouts.

Being a Partner with Adults

With your co-leader or assistant leaders:

☐ You share in planning each adult's part in future meetings.

☐ You evaluate the troop's progress and work toward balanced activities and opportunities for each girl.

☐ You explore ways to tackle problems that occur in the troop.

☐ You identify needs for additional time, talents, and skills that might be supplied by other adults or by older Girl Scouts.

☐ You find ways of getting these people to help you.

☐ You make exploratory visits and set up arrangements for troop trips and camping.

☐ You keep your adult teammates informed of Girl Scout events, training opportunities, and resources.

With other adults close to the troop:

☐ You consult with parents or guardians of the girls and keep them informed about troop meetings, schedules, special events, plans, and progress.

☐ You seek help from your troop committee (see page 28 of this book) for things the girls need, such as equipment, materials, and transportation.

☐ You draw on the talents and community contacts of all these interested adults.

With adults in the community:

☐ You seek community resource people to help you and the girls with program activities.

☐ You link troop activities with those of appropriate community groups and organizations.

For more about working with adults, see "Getting Help to Do Your Job," pages 28-29 of this leaders' guide.

Being Accountable

As troop leader, you are responsible for keeping records of troop activities and finances.

Together with the girls involved, you decide when requirements for a specific recognition have been fulfilled.

You register all girls and adults in the troop as members of the Girl Scout movement.

You keep your Girl Scout council informed of troop activities, needs, and accomplishments.

(See the resource list at the end of this book for aids to record keeping.)

Learning and Growing

Girl Scouting offers many aids to effective leadership. It is your responsibility to use them.

You keep yourself informed through council bulletins or newsletters and the *Girl Scout Leader* magazine.

You share with and learn from other leaders through training and leadership events offered by your council or other community groups.

You seek help when you need it for developing skills or examining problems. See pages 28-29 of this book.

Getting into Action on Activities

It's fun for Brownie and Junior age girls to think up ideas for activities. It's even more fun to do them. Usually, the younger the girl the less time she wants to linger over planning what to do, and the sooner she wants to be involved in the doing. For girls six through eleven, getting into action quickly and enjoyably is the name of the game.

Here are some tips and how-to's for helping girls move into—and through—action.

Use the girls' handbook and the guidelines for building a good atmosphere on page 16 of this leaders' guide.

Exploring and Collecting Activity Ideas

Ideas for program activities come from the girls' interests, experiences, and imagination □ from their wishes, hopes, and expectations □ from handbook suggestions and things other Girl Scouts have done before □ from everywhere in the girl's world.

Collecting Ideas. You will find some useful suggestions on this subject in the handbook. Here are some other ways to try:

Talking together in Brownie Ring (or in Junior patrols or interest groups), listing ideas on big charts as they arise.

Partner "Interviews." Girls pair off, and each girl finds out what her partner would like the troop to do; then partners report to the whole group on each other's suggestions.

Handbook Hunts. At home or in troop meeting, each person looks through the handbook for: things that would be fun to do indoors, outdoors, with other girls, by herself, with_____ □ something she has done before □ something new she would like to try □ something that costs little or nothing to do □ something from each of the five Worlds □ and so on.

"Ten-mile Hike." Set out ten numbered items to stimulate activity ideas. These could be magazine or calendar photos, or objects related to activities in the Worlds of program. In teams, girls go from one item to another to see how many activity ideas they can draw from looking at or handling each item. Stress "things you would like to do." (See Kim's Game on page 105 of the handbook as a possible variation.)

Show and Tell. Girls bring things to show as they tell of their own interests.

You might also:

Do an activity or two from the handbook, and see how many spin-off ideas you can gather. (See page 21 of this leaders' guide for how one idea can lead to many others.)

Have a "taster" meeting, indoors or out, in which girls rotate from one short activity to another, discovering the flavor of lots of different program possibilities. (An idea from each World, perhaps?) You need other adults or older girls to help with various activities.

Make the "taster" a wide game (see page 60 in this book).

Tips to Remember

Girls often express their activity preferences in broad, rather vague terms: "going places" □ "learning to cook" □ "making something" □ "sing" □ "find out about..." □ "play games" □ "do something for little children." They may have specifics in mind, but they may need help to pin these down.

Almost no idea is so far-fetched, so wild that it might not, with some creative effort, become a real activity. Acknowledge every girl's ideas and interests as valuable.

Use troop government structures and processes (Brownie Ring, Junior patrol system) to help in gathering ideas. The fairness built into these helps assure each girl a chance to express and explore ideas before choices are made.

Things to Watch For

As girls gather ideas, see that:

they are encouraged to build on each other's ideas, asking questions, adding dimensions.

choices are not limited to things that you like or can teach. Take a chance! Show that you are willing to learn something new along with the girls.

Making Choices

When there are lots of things to choose from, choice may not be easy, especially for girls who have not had many choice-making experiences.

You can help by:

pointing out how ideas and interests can combine into activities. (For younger girls, you may have to show them how it is done—grouping their ideas together into suggested projects. Girl Scout patches, badges, and signs are designed to arrange activities in ways that make choices easier.)

identifying short-term and longer-term activities. Girls want some things to do at once, and some that they can plan for later.

clearly stating what it is the girls are deciding about:

> We're choosing between (activity) and (activity).
>
> Everyone is choosing the idea she likes best.
>
> We are deciding which one of these things we want to do first.
>
> We are choosing which things we want to do together as a troop.

suggesting alternatives if the girls can't decide. (Allow time, think it over at home, talk it over with others.)

using aids to choosing: raised hand (with or without eyes covered), voice vote, secret ballot if decisions are close or girls want it.

assuring girls that ideas not used right away will be saved for another time. (Some ways to do this are a dream box, idea scrapbook, or file girls can create and refer to.)

Tips to Remember

Alas, there aren't many shortcuts in learning to make wise decisions. The only way to do it is by making a number of decisions and examining the results. Expect some confusion, hesitancy, changes of mind.

It's easier at first to select from just two or three activities.

Older or more experienced girls are likely to compromise or go along with what most others (or special friends) want to do. Younger ones may cling to "what I want to do" as the main basis for their choice.

Deciding on activities that the whole troop will do together calls for grappling with the problems and joys of diversity in a group (differences of age, interest, ability, experience). Help girls see ways to include each other's interests and desires. Avoid solving the problem for them.

As girls choose, see if:

Choosing is doing. Is it active and fun? Do you and the girls get to know each other better—discover talents, interests, skills, expectations—in the process of making choices?

Girls are talking about how to do activities, along with their choice of what they will do. This helps assure that activities will meet expectations, and sets the stage for planning.

Planning What to Do

Some activities that girls choose can be done almost immediately, with little or no planning. Others will require some thinking through, some more decisions on "how," some looking ahead and organizing.

When you help girls plan, you help them discover how to move from idea to action and feel the satisfaction that comes with "doing it ourselves."

You can help by:

using processes of troop government and decision making to involve everyone who needs to be involved in the plans, to divide the work to be done so that everyone does her part to make a plan succeed.

being aware of the girls' capabilities and moving at a speed that is comfortable to them.

giving practical pointers. Girls may not think of cost, how long something will take, people to help, transportation, equipment.

guiding planning in small enough steps that girls can see parts of a plan working right away.

making an agreement as to what parts you (or other adults) will do, and what parts girls will do.

working with individual girls, or with committees or patrols, to help them develop their parts of a plan. You provide encouragement and help with skills or resources.

using visual ways to summarize needs and actions, to show a plan growing as you go along. For example:

Job	Time Needed	Who Will Do?	Equipment & Materials	Cost	Special Reminders

Tips to Remember

Planning doesn't happen all at once. Intersperse planning times with songs, games, or other activities.

Inexperienced planners do better with short-term plans—considering the What, Where, When, Who, for only a few meetings ahead.

A big calendar, with holidays, special Girl Scout events, and major projects, lets everyone see what's ahead and helps planners fit activities into the time available.

A rainy day or an unplanned absence can upset plans unless girls have allowed for possible mishaps. Help the girls to anticipate, to consider the "what—if's" (no need to dwell on possible horrors, but do look at realistic, life's-like-that possibilities and get the jump on them).

As girls plan, see that:

They have up-to-the-elbows involvement, not just finger-tip contact while you do the real planning.

Everyone knows her part of a plan and how she fits into the total picture.

Planning is doing, a process, not a thing: as you plan, get resource materials, investigate costs firsthand, juggle time, use calendars, charts, checklists, interview a prospective activity consultant, visit the site of a proposed trip.

Carrying Out Activities and Projects

Carrying out planned activities is *doing* in its most recognizable form.

You can help girls to:

Enjoy to the fullest.

Discover and use new skills and knowledge.

Apply their talents and abilities to new situations.

Realize that things don't always come out the way they were planned; make needed adjustments, be creative in handling surprises, and learn from mistakes.

Tips to Remember

Guard the health and safety of the girls. Help them heighten their own safety-consciousness, watching for signs of fatigue or upset. Girls' doing things for themselves does not extend to situations that represent clear danger of physical or emotional injury. There may be times when, for their protection, you will have to step in.

You can help girls recognize and talk about learnings, accomplishments, and the results of good and poor planning while an activity is in progress. Real evaluation starts when an activity begins, not when it ends.

Evaluating Learnings and Experience

Evaluating an experience is a way to focus on learnings and prepare for future action. After an activity is over, evaluation usually happens naturally: on the way home, as girls gather at the next troop meeting, as plans for another activity begin.

You can help by:

talking with girls about both positive and negative experiences: why they had fun □ how their plans worked □ what they enjoyed the most □ what didn't work so well □ things they didn't like □ what they would do differently another time.

pointing out connections between goals and the ways planned to achieve them. If expectations were not met, what could be done next time to make sure they will be?

focusing on learnings and accomplishments of girls— not just successes and problems of the activity.

Share "Something I/we discovered"(about me, about others, about _____).

Share "Something I/we learned to do" (better, for the first time).

Share "Some ways I/we can use what I/we learned."

This is an opportunity to help girls recognize each other's skills and contributions.

celebrating. Sing. Create a song or poem about the activity or event. Start a scrapbook or add to one. Share highlights of the activity with parents, friends, school, other troops, your Girl Scout council.

Blazing a Program Trail

Collect some ideas. Girls pick the ones they like best. Together, you and the girls weave these ideas into a plan. The plan might be for next week or several weeks. Then carry it through.

This is the start of the adventure of blazing a program trail.

As the troop develops projects around interests and ideals in the handbook, some program trails will be short and some will be long. You will find that spin-offs from any activity in a World could take part of one meeting or even a year. The possibilities in the handbook are almost endless.

Tasting: trying a new skill or sampling activities could lead to...

Exploring and discovering: uncovering *how*, finding out *why*, learning about people, places, things, ideas...

Sharing: showing others, learning from them, doing things together.

All this can go on and on, as each idea sparks a new project. Girls bring their own experiences and interests to Girl Scouting. Let the handbook be a starting point for building and expanding on these through creative and adventuresome program.

Allow ideas to flow, even ideas that sometimes seem beyond your reach. Sometimes a simple idea can grow into an exciting new experience.

Here is a diagram of how a program trail might develop. Remember, in Girl Scouting each group blazes its own trail.

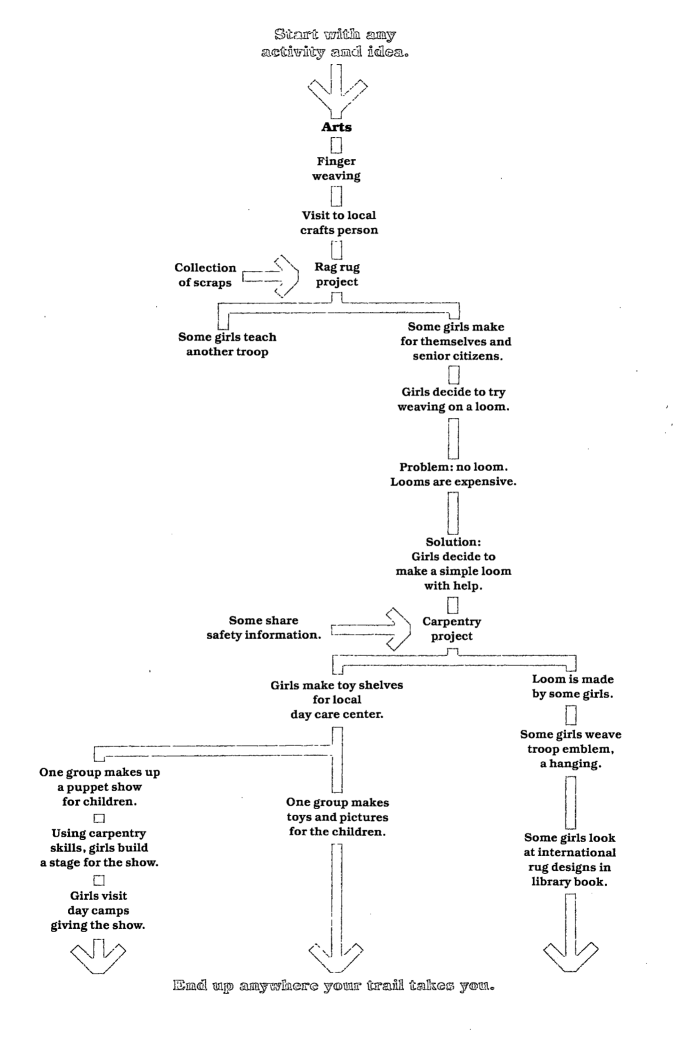

Start with any
activity and idea.

Arts

Finger
weaving

Visit to local
crafts person

Collection
of scraps → Rag rug
project

Some girls teach
another troop

Some girls make
for themselves and
senior citizens.

Girls decide to try
weaving on a loom.

Problem: no loom.
Looms are expensive.

Solution:
Girls decide to
make a simple loom
with help.

Some share
safety information. → Carpentry
project

Girls make toy shelves
for local
day care center.

Loom is made
by some girls.

One group makes up
a puppet show
for children.

Using carpentry
skills, girls build
a stage for the show.

Girls visit
day camps
giving the show.

One group makes
toys and pictures
for the children.

Some girls weave
troop emblem,
a hanging.

Some girls look
at international
rug designs in
library book.

End up anywhere your trail takes you.

What other things might be happening in this troop?

Special Girl Scout Days:[1]

Juliette Low's Birthday, October 31

Thinking Day, February 22

Girl Scout Birthday, March 12

Girl Scout Week, the week including March 12

Special Ceremonies:[2]

investiture ceremony

rededication or fly-up ceremony

Court of Awards

Scouts' Own

flag ceremonies

Other Activities and Projects:

patch, badge, or sign activities for groups and individuals

picnics, outings, troop camping

community service projects

visits and invited guests

health, safety, and first aid practice

---

[1]See handbook pages 29-31.

[2]See handbook pages 31-39.

Planning for Balanced Girl Scout Program

Record what the troop does during the troop year by writing brief notes on activities in the appropriate boxes.
Use this chart as you help girls plan a well-rounded variety of activities.

	World of Well-Being	World of People	World of Today and Tomorrow	World of the Arts	World of the Out-of-Doors
Participated in short-term activities					
Gained and applied new skills and/or information					
Planned and carried out a project or event					
Took a trip away from the meeting place					
Gave service					
Participated in an intertroop or council activity— with other troop(s), in neighborhood, district, or councilwide					
Explored vocational/ avocational opportunities					

Some Basic Techniques for Girl Involvement and Action

There are many ways to do almost anything. These form a reservoir of possibilities for each activity. Subject matter, girls' interests, time, money, and equipment, all determine the combinations you will choose.

Some Techniques:
Discussion
Brainstorming
Acting Out
Trips and Visits
Games
Arts

No list is ever complete. The more you and the girls add on your own, the more you enrich the program. Girls are good at thinking up fun ways to do activities; in fact, they come up with some of the best.

What can your troop add to the list?

Discussion

Discussions take place all the time. Whenever people get together and talk, they share ideas, new and old.

In a good discussion:
Everyone is involved.
It gathers its own steam; people keep talking.
It is exciting.
Arguments sometimes happen.
If there is a leader, she stays in the background.

If the girls seem uninvolved, you can spark things by asking a thought-provoking question related to their experiences. Questions with "yes" and "no" answers or "right" and "wrong" answers can stop the talking. Try open-ended questions with many possible answers, such as:

What do you like best about....?
What would you do if....?
What would you like to do....?
How was this activity different from the last one....?

Some Tips for Discussion

Try not to let one person or a group take over. (This includes adults.) Occasionally, go "around the circle" and give everyone a turn to talk.
Break the discussion with a quick, active song or game if girls are fidgety and restless.

Help girls generate new ideas and real sharing. Let the girls do the talking.
A circle or other informal seating arrangement (on the floor) can help participation.
As girls gain experience, help them to take turns being the discussion leader.

Brainstorming

A special kind of discussion, which can be used to collect a number of ideas quickly, is brainstorming. Imagination is the secret of brainstorming; practicality and logic don't count.

There are a few simple rules:
All ideas are welcome without criticism. (Criticism can come later.)
The wilder the idea the better. (Ideas can be toned down later.)
Quantity of ideas is what is needed. (Quality can come later, when ideas are sorted.)

Piggybacking of ideas is welcome. (Combine your own thought with something that has been said, or add onto another person's idea.)

The group will need a recorder, someone who can write fast to keep up with the rush of ideas you hope will come.

The subject for brainstorming can be written on a blackboard or on a large piece of paper. Then you're ready to go, and the point is to go fast. Don't try to keep it up for more than 15 or 20 minutes; it is important to stop before the ideas dry up.

If nobody wants to speak first, try going around the circle in turn. A girl either speaks up quickly or says, "I pass."

Agree on a noisy signal—ringing a bell, pounding a table, or whatever appeals to the girls—for the discussion leader to use whenever someone makes a comment like "That won't work." Anything negative is out of bounds in brainstorming.

When the recorder has collected as many ideas as you think the group can handle, stop brainstorming and take a look at what you have. Ask the girls to identify ideas the troop can use, ideas that won't work, and ideas that might turn into something great if developed.

Acting Out

Acting out feelings and situations can help children discover more about themselves and others. Girls can pretend to become and feel like people in particular situations, acting alone or with other players, making up words and actions as they go. Role playing, improvisation, pantomime, or puppets can be used. Later, as they talk about it, they explore how they felt and what happened in different roles.

Role playing is very useful in imagining a new situation, or in learning how to act or do something. For instance, girls can act out situations for the Girl Scout Law, or to practice being a patrol leader, or to show what might happen when a guest arrives.

Role-Playing Tips:

Define the situation and the roles to be acted out.

Keep the situation simple.

Don't force anyone to role play.

Be flexible; things can go in many directions.

Avoid role playing when a person is emotionally upset about a subject.

Trips and Visits

Taking trips that are based on girls' interests can broaden their world. Girls love to go places and there are ways to plan trips in every community, no matter how large or small.

Visit members of the community with skills to share or stories to tell.

Visit local institutions and businesses, from the local firehouse or museum to a neighboring farm, mill, or plant.

A parent/guardian could arrange a visit to his or her place of work.

A visit to someone's home can be exciting, and sharing things like new puppies, a carpentry workshop, or baking bread are always fun.

Go for a walk, or just step outside, to explore. It is active, fun, and a break in routine.

As girls get older, overnight trips can be planned. Larger cities or rural areas are fascinating to girls who did not grow up there. Check your council rules regarding overnight trips or traveling considerable distances.

Be prepared in advance. Permission slips are required if your troop meets away from its regular meeting place.

Besides regular visiting hours, museums and other public places often have special rules for large groups. Don't just go there, or you might not be admitted.

It is important to make arrangements in advance for visits to people at home or at work. A briefing on what the troop has been doing and what especially interests the girls will make the visit more rewarding for everyone.

Let the girls know about preliminaries that make for a successful trip. See if some of them would like to take responsibility for gathering information that is needed.

Before you go, be sure you are familiar with all of the Girl Scout standards for trips; you'll find them in *Safety-Wise.*

Games

Often children are more receptive to an activity if they see it in the form of a game.

A game can be used or created for almost any occasion. Some games are physical, some verbal, and some written. Some are combinations of these.

A discussion can become a game if you pass a "talking stick" around. Only the person holding the stick can talk. Sometimes passing a ball of yarn from person to person encourages girls to talk; if each person keeps hold of her part of the yarn and passes the ball along, a pattern of participation grows.

Guessing games can be based on new skills, safety rules, or whatever you like. Each group can make up its own questions and ask others. Examples: "What would you do if your buddy wanted to go swimming and you didn't" or "You get a cut and you are in the woods...." Answers can be stated or acted out.

Schoolyard games make good physical activities. Your girls probably know quite a few. Relays, for example, can be adapted to most any subject.

See The World of Well-Being in the handbook for more games and sports, and for ideas on making up games.

Arts

The World of the Arts includes drama, music, dance, and reading and writing, as well as the visual arts.

Girls can use arts to say how they feel □ to tell a story of what happened □ to describe something □ to teach someone □ as a model to use later □ just for fun.

The arts can be used as self-expression for any part of an activity. Use them in getting ideas and making choices □ as a main activity □ for remembering, evaluating, and celebrating.

Arts are useful everywhere: indoors, outdoors, on the way to somewhere else. They make an activity out of something inactive. For example, drawing pictures or show and tell makes for a much livelier evaluation than formal discussion.

Try keeping a few supplies on hand at all times: a songbook, paper and crayons, paste, yarn, and scissors. Then you can be ready at a moment's notice.

See The World of the Arts section, pages 49-56, in this leaders' guide and The World of the Arts chapter in the girls' handbook.

Troop Meetings

Things to Consider

When: once a week for one to two hours.

Who: girls of different ages, grades, and backgrounds.

enough girls to provide group activities but still meet individual needs.

an adult leader and an assistant leader.

program consultants.

Where: location accessible to all members.

safe, clean place.

large enough area for group activities.

first aid equipment available.

What: girl-adult planning.

activities in five Worlds of program: Well-Being, People, Today and Tomorrow, Out-of-Doors, Arts.

interaction with other troops.

participation in the community.

Trips, Visits, and Camping

Participation in outdoor and community activities determined by needs, interests, and readiness of girls.

Health and safety standards in *Safety-Wise* followed.

Necessary permissions obtained.

Two adults for any group of 12 Brownies or 16 Juniors. One adult for each additional 6 Brownies and 8 Juniors.

Special Considerations

Opinions and practices of all cultural and religious groups in membership respected.

Provisions made for handicapped girls.

Money-earning projects chosen according to guidelines in Program Standards (page 90 of this book).

Regard for others at and away from meeting place.

More detailed guidelines are given in the Program Standards, pages 87-91 of this guide.

Ingredients of a Troop Meeting

This is a sample of a meeting. Adapt it as you choose. The only necessary part is some major activity; even dues collection may be put off if the group is going on a trip or doing a service project elsewhere. Share this list of ingredients with the girls, and see how it compares with what they expect a meeting to be.

Pre-Meeting Activity

Opener

Business (at any point)

Major Activities

Planning (any time)

Closing

Pre-Meeting Activity—Suggestions

Posting kaper chart and any news.

Setting out chairs and materials.

Decorating room.

Simple project or game.

Mix and talk.

Tips to Leaders

Girls may participate as they arrive.

Group unity increases as members arrive.

Disruptions will occur as girls arrive.

Can be kept informal.

Collection of dues and attendance, permissions, etc., can be handled individually, as girls arrive (or by patrol leaders).

Opener—Suggestions

Songs, games, skits.

An activity from one of the Worlds.

An idea session.

A ceremony.

A surprise.

Tips to Leaders

Girls usually gather together as a group.

Depending upon the girls, they might start the opener, or you might need to give the cue.

A high-interest activity is useful.

See "Ceremonies for Girl Scouts" in the handbook.

Business (at any point)— Suggestions

Old business.

Collection of dues and treasurer's report.

Sharing of calendar—new dates, invitations, cookie sale, special events.

Tips to Leaders

Be brief and simple.

Usually as large group. Juniors often collect dues in patrols.

Leader often coordinates, or coordination by girls can be rotated to help develop leadership skills.

Major Activities—Suggestions

New activities from Worlds.

Action on patches, badges, signs.

Work on ongoing project (e.g., community, nature, arts).

Outside speaker (visitor).

Presentation or show by girls or others.

Party.

Visit, trip out-of-doors.

Tips to Leaders

This is the crux of the meeting for the girl. It is in her active participation that she gains a sense of what she can and cannot do.

To avoid frustration and a sense of defeat, aim towards activities that girls can enjoy and feel successful at.

Troop activities should let each girl learn new skills and use old ones, with both people and things.

The choice of how to form groups for activities can come from the girls. Vary the ways of grouping.

Major activity can happen with a large group, an interest group or patrols, or individually, depending upon circumstances.

If interest lags for a group or an individual, help them shift into another activity or view what they are doing in a different light.

If you encounter frustration in an individual or the group, look at the situation and determine whether the group needs more support or is just not ready to handle it. If necessary, help the girls modify their plans and substitute something more appropriate.

Evaluate the activity with the girls, emphasizing the why and how.

Reminder: Girls often need more time than adults; be flexible and let them have fun.

Have something up your sleeve in case girls finish early or need a change of pace. Draw on your own skills to teach a song, share something new, repeat something old and successful.

Be prepared for anything!

Planning (any time)—Suggestions

Planning, deciding, and reviewing Brownie Ring or committees.

Junior patrols and Court of Honor or other form of troop government.

Troop decisions.

Tips to Leaders

Planning is flexible; the group can plan more than once at a meeting, depending upon mood.

The beginning of a meeting is a good time to pick up on any planning needed for the rest of the meeting and for ongoing projects.

In the meetings before big events, planning becomes the major activity.

Discuss, rap, brainstorm on past or future activities, in small groups.

After groups have come to agreement, they report to the whole group (or Court of Honor), decisions are made, and girls are ready to move into the major activity.

Days with a lot of planning need balance with short, active games or other physical activities.

Closing—Suggestions

Wrap-up and reminders.

Sharing of new plans and responsibilities.

Song or game.

Ceremony.

Clean-up.

Tips to Leaders

Girls regroup to share experiences and reactions. Leave time for questions.

A final decision on a plan for the next meeting might be made here.

Time for review of unfinished business and remembering commitments (such as permission slips, supplies, dues, telephoning someone) made for future meetings.

Gives girls a chance to talk.

A time to slow down, wind down.

Cleanup may be done before or after the closing. This is the girls' responsibility; make sure you leave time for it. Cleanup itself can be rotated or made into a group game.

Cleanup might be the responsibility of a certain patrol or group.

Problem Solving with Girls

Within any group, there will be problems from time to time, and a Girl Scout troop is no exception. Resolving problems through conversation is an art that is slowly learned. With your help girls can develop skill in this art. Working in partnership, you and the girls may need to face and resolve problems of individual behavior and interpersonal relationships. Sometimes you will be working out problems with the whole troop. Other times you will need to deal with one patrol or group or privately with one individual.

Since each situation is different, there is no easy formula to follow. Here are some steps to consider:

1 What is the real problem?
2 What are some possible reasons it exists/happened?
3 What are possible solutions?
4 What are possible consequences?
5 Agreement on solution.

Here are some hints for using these problem-solving steps.

1 What is the real problem?
Problems may just pop up, or girls may come to you with problems.

The real problem may be obvious, or it may be hidden by anger, fear, confusion, frustration, etc. Help girls to peel away the feelings until the real problem can be seen.

Girls may hesitate to say what the real problem is, fearing to look foolish or selfish or to cause displeasure. Help them to see the importance of expressing feelings.

You may be aware of a problem that the girls have not acknowledged.

First, ask yourself: "Is it only a problem to me?" Perhaps it's just a sign of healthy development like questioning authority or blowing off steam.

A direct approach helps. You might say:

"It looks as if we have a problem here that we need to work on together."

"(situation) seems to be causing difficulties. Let's try to figure out what is wrong."

"You seem to be unhappy. How can I (or we) help?"

2 What are some possible reasons?
Encourage girls to explore many possible reasons for a situation. Ask: "Why do you think this happened?"

Resist the temptation to settle for simple explanations. (For example: "It's all Sue's fault for being so stubborn."..."We would have had fun if it hadn't rained.") Say:

"That's one possibility. What might be some others?"

Things bogged down? Deadly silence? Tears? Some reasons can't be discovered quickly. Suggest taking time to think things over.

Emotions may be very strong. Encourage girls to express feelings as well as facts. Take time to hear, and try to understand: "I'm angry because she (they)..."..."It's not fair that..."

Be willing to look at what you are doing, too, and make needed adjustments.

Behavior that distresses you might be a sign of boredom.

Girls may be too polite to say that activities are repetitious, that they lack chances for real action, self-expression, and a feeling of accomplishment.

Through listening and action, show girls that you are open to their suggestions and concerned about their needs and happiness.

3 What are possible solutions?
Help girls think of as many possible solutions as they can.

Encourage action that involves personal responsibility, not just direction for what other people should do. Ask:

"What do you think are some fair ways you might settle this (make the situation better, improve the way we...)?"

"How would you like to handle this?"

"What do you think I could do? What could you do?"

4 What are possible consequences?
Help girls consider the consequences of solutions they suggest. Ask:

"If I (or we) did that, what might happen?"

"Would that work, do you think?"

Focus on handling a situation, not a person. Ask:

"What can we do to be sure everyone is enjoying...?"

NOT

"What should we do about Cindy?"

5 Agreement on solution.
Agree on a solution everyone involved will try, and try it.

A solution is like a plan: state the goal, what action is agreed upon, who will do what, when and how.

Avoid the temptation to manipulate decisions so that they will come out the way you want them to.

If the solution agreed upon doesn't work, help the girls modify it and try again.

Dealing with Behavior Crises

Occasionally, there may be situations in which you will have to act first and explain later. Sympathetic firmness and encouragement are more useful than lectures or threats for helping girls learn to control their own behavior.

Unsafe Behavior. When a girl's actions pose a threat of physical injury to herself or others, you must step in quickly and firmly. Then you can remind girls that, as their leader, you are responsible for their safety in the troop. If it seems appropriate, explain why the situation or action was unsafe.

Temper Tantrums. Many six-through-eleven-year-olds lose their tempers easily. Usually, such anger is short-lived. But real temper tantrums require adult intervention.

A girl who cannot handle her anger or hostility is often frightened of her lack of self-control.

Move her away from the group to some quiet place until she calms down. Stay with her for a while and talk quietly if she feels like talking. Let the girl know that you recognize how scary it can be when feelings get out of control.

Your co-leader or another adult helper should continue activities with the rest of the group. Point out to the other girls that keeping angry feelings under control is difficult, and that (girl's name) needs a chance to work on this until she feels she can rejoin the group.

Cruel Teasing. Young children do a lot of teasing. It's a natural part of testing each other and themselves. Cruel "scapegoating" that continues unchecked can be emotionally harmful to both the girl teased and those who do the teasing.

Let the girls know that you cannot stand by and let them be inconsiderate or cruel. Remind them that it takes hard work to live by the Girl Scout Promise. It is in relationships with others that "I will try" and "I will do my best" are put to the toughest test.

Destructiveness. Show girls that you will not allow destructive mischief, cruel treatment of things in the natural environment, or mistreatment of the belongings of others.

I will not let you hurt this cat (dog, rabbit, garden, etc.).

I expect you to take better care of (the troop's belongings, Mary's sweater, etc.).

Disruptiveness. When repeated acts of disruption spoil things for others, indicate that there are limits. Point out that you cannot permit one person to keep the other girls from having fun. If the group gets noisy in a museum, remind them that other people are entitled to enjoy their visit, too.

Asking a girl to "decide whether she will work with the group or leave the meeting" may help—if there is some safe place she can go should she decide to leave. Another place in the room, or another room may do; but don't let her leave the meeting place unless you can contact a parent or guardian who will be responsible for her safety.

Getting Help to Do Your Job

In Girl Scouting, you'll find all kinds of help when you need it. Both the handbook and this leaders' guide mention a number of resources that can lighten your tasks as a leader and make the troop's activities more varied and enjoyable.

Here is a review of different ways you can go about getting help.

People

Your best resource, always, is people. When you think of getting someone to help you, don't just look for experts. Many other people can be helpful in troop projects.

Girls. Troop members and their friends may know a person who has just the knowledge or equipment you need. Older Girl Scouts can be very helpful in teaching skills and sharing knowledge of Girl Scout ways.

Families. Get to know the parents or guardians of troop members as soon as you can, so that they can be aware of and support the Girl Scout activities. An adult meeting or a party with the girls, after the troop has made some initial plans, can show parents what is going on and encourage them to help. If you are ready with a list of specific things they could do for the troop, and can get a commitment from each person to do one job, you're really on your way. Older sisters and brothers can often make a contribution, too.

Neighbors. Many of the people you and the girls come in contact with can be helpful to the troop. Senior citizens have much knowledge, skill, and experience to share.

Young professional people are often eager to share their special interests with children. Look for hobbyists as well as people with unusual occupations; you may find them in your own backyard. Helping girls to meet and work with as many new adults as possible will broaden their experience, make life easier for you, and offer the troop more exciting things to do.

The Girl Scout Organization

Girl Scouting is people, of course—and a lot of these people have jobs specifically related to yours. Ultimately, all jobs in the Girl Scout organization exist to serve the girls and leaders in troops.

Your Girl Scout Council

If you live in one of the fifty states, or in the District of Columbia, the Canal Zone, Guam, or Puerto Rico, your troop is located in a Girl Scout council, one of about 350 councils in the United States. The council has been chartered by Girl Scouts of the U.S.A. to organize and maintain Girl Scouting in a certain geographic area. It is run by volunteer representatives from local areas—a board of directors and volunteer committees—who give direction to other volunteers and a paid staff. Councils draw their financial support from local communities through appeals such as the United Way and through supplementary fund raising, most often cookie sales and Sustaining Membership Enrollment.

Councils vary in their structure and in the titles they give to different functions. All of them, however, provide certain basic services.

Direct services to troops. Groups of people in each part of the council area organize troops, recruit leaders, and act as consultants to leaders. A consultant, usually an experienced troop leader, may help you as you start your leadership job. She can give you individualized guidance as you go along, by visiting to talk over the troop's progress and problems, and also help you to take part in activities of the council.

Your consultant or organizer can help you to start a troop committee. This is a group of three to six adults whose purpose is to help you and the girls put program ideas into action. Troop committee members—parents, guardians, friends, a member of the troop's sponsoring group, anyone who cares about young people—can help you with equipment, record-keeping, transportation, and other needs of the troop.

Support services. The council develops and maintains the quality of Girl Scouting in its area. It handles financial and business matters related to Girl Scouting within the council jurisdiction. Some of the services usually provided by councils are:

o training for leaders, both new and experienced

o camps for use of girls in the council

o councilwide events for girls and leaders

o materials such as books, magazines, audiovisual aids, and perhaps some equipment for troop use

o a council bulletin or newsletter

Your National Girl Scout Organization

Girl Scouts of the U.S.A. is chartered by Congress to develop and maintain Girl Scouting nationally. The organization's governing body is a National Council made up of delegates from every council in the United States. Assembling every three years in a national convention, this representative group elects a National Board of Directors, sets policies to be followed by everyone in Girl Scouting, and in general gives direction to the movement in this country.

The organization employs a national staff to pool experiences of Girl Scouts throughout the United States and to provide services to members. Some of the services are explained under "Membership and Registration" on page 12 of this leaders' guide.

When you register as an adult in Girl Scouting, you automatically become a subscriber to the *Girl Scout Leader* magazine. Every issue brings you a sense of contact with people, happenings, and the spirit of Girl Scouting across the nation. News of projects and announcements of new materials, as well as how-to-do-it program helps, come to you through the *Leader* magazine.

Research, development, and training activities of the national organization benefit you through your own Girl Scout council.

The national Girl Scout organization is also your link with the World Association of Girl Guides and Girl Scouts. Through the national Juliette Low World Friendship Fund (page 46 of this book), Brownies and Juniors can contribute to the work of Girl Guiding and Girl Scouting around the world. Ideas for troop participation in Thinking Day and other celebrations with an international flavor come to you through GSUSA publications.

Check the resource list at the end of this book and the Girl Scout publications catalog for books and pamphlets published especially to help you with specific parts of the Girl Scout program and with your job as a leader.

Other Organizations and Agencies

Many local community groups are eager to work with Girl Scouting for the benefit of youth. Some of them in your community might be:

libraries	other youth-serving agencies
churches, synagogues, and temples	professional groups
schools	parks and zoos
women's groups	environmental groups
utility companies	businesses
museums	unions
Chamber of Commerce	local clubs and hobby groups
	service sororities

You and the girls can ask these organizations and agencies for advice about projects or for free materials related to the troop's interests. Check with your Girl Scout council first, though; they may have already done the legwork. Watch the council bulletin for announcements of resources offered by other community groups.

Also consider national resources: government agencies such as state and federal Agriculture Extension Services, and large organizations that may have local units near you—for example, American Red Cross, National Council of Negro Women, and League of United Latin American Citizens (LULAC).

Materials

Many kinds of material can add interest to Girl Scout activities: books, pamphlets, slides, films, calendars, posters, photographs, newspapers, and magazines. Keep your eyes open for good ones, and encourage girls to share appropriate materials that they may find at home, at school, or in other groups they belong to.

Check the public library, your own home, and the Girl Scout council office for materials the troop can use.

Use the resource list in this leaders' guide, page 79, to get you started on the search for new ideas.

Helping Yourself

Keep yourself informed on what is happening to young people in your community and beyond. Check schools, libraries, and bookstores to see what girls are reading; read some of these books and magazines yourself. Watch some children's TV shows. Pay attention to young people as they speak and question and interact in the troop, and everywhere else.

Talk with other adults who work with children in both formal and informal settings: teachers, religious leaders, club and sports leaders. Share your leadership experiences with other Girl Scout leaders at meetings, workshops, and problem clinics as well as in leadership courses.

Evaluate your own leadership periodically. Focus on your strengths and talents, then assess what else you need to know, understand, or practice to be a more effective leader. (This is a good time to use "Some Guidelines for Measuring Progress," page 76 of this leaders' guide.) Be honest— and don't be too hard on yourself.

Ask for help when you need it. Be aware of where to get it, and learn how to "yell for help" effectively.

The Handbook: Introduction to Girl Scouting

The opening chapter of the handbook tells a girl what Girl Scouting is, how it works, and what makes it unique. It also tells her what is special about her level of Girl Scouting, whether she is a Brownie or a Junior.

Instead of repeating the information at an adult level, this leaders' guide gives you additional information and suggestions keyed to material in the handbook. You will find explanations, fuller details, and additional activity ideas that you need to help girls translate the written word into action.

Suzy Safety

(handbook page 5)

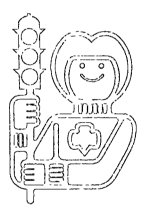

Wherever an activity with potential safety hazards is pictured in the handbook, the figure of Suzy Safety appears. Encourage Brownies and Juniors to spot Suzy and to say what the hazard is in each case. You will also want to discover the best way of avoiding these hazards. If girls know the answer without your telling them—fine! Use your copy of *Safety-Wise*, the official Girl Scout safety manual, as a guide to safety practices in all troop activities.

Try a safety hike at day camp, or when you are troop camping on a council-owned site. Girls can find places that might be dangerous and post pictures of Suzy Safety to warn other campers.

More information on health and safety is scattered through the handbook (expecially The World of Well-Being); also see pages 40-43 of this leaders' guide.

Becoming a Girl Scout

(handbook page 6)

See the section on ceremonies in this leaders' guide (pages 32-35).

The Promise and Law

(handbook page 7)

Acceptance of the Girl Scout Promise is a qualification of membership in the Girl Scout movement. However, Brownies and Juniors may not fully understand the Promise they make. It is often hard for them to relate the abstract words of the Promise to the everyday world around them or to a code for living. In the handbook, an attempt has been made to help young girls understand what the Girl Scout Promise and Law means in action. They will need help from you, too.

With Brownies, *do*, rather than talk about. Act out, sing songs, do art. Relate the Promise and Law to the Brownie B's and to the Brownie story on page 49 of the handbook. Do not expect girls of this age to memorize the Law.

With Juniors also, action is the key. Activities related to understanding and using the Promise and Law are part of a number of badge and sign requirements. Juniors can see how using this code can make troop government more effective.

Encourage girls to recognize acts that demonstrate a girl's effort to live by the code she has accepted. Try not to use the Promise and Law only for pointing out misbehavior. Help each girl to use this code as a tool for personal guidance, not as a weapon against others or herself.

Understanding the Girl Scout Promise

Help the girls to share their understanding of what a promise means. (Don't be surprised if it means something different to every child.) One way to approach the concept of a promise is to have each girl make up a promise about her own daily life. (For example, "I promise to be as nice as I can to my baby brother all week." "I promise to take very good care of my puppy." Or maybe, "I promise not to repeat anything that anybody tells me as a secret.")

Afterwards the girls could share their promises with each other. Remember, all are valid. Each promise comes from what is important to the girl at that time. Telling others is, in itself, an act of commitment. The individual promises could then be compared to the Girl Scout Promise, which says how Girl Scouts will try to live their lives every day. Help the girls make realistic promises that they can keep with a reasonable amount of effort, so they can feel successful. Stress "I will try" rather than perfection.

Understanding the Girl Scout Law

You might discuss with the girls what laws are and how they are created. You could talk about government in and outside the troop, how people cooperate with each other, and how they try to use the democratic process in making and following laws. Younger girls can explore how the members of a family can help each other; or how rules, such as safety rules, are there to help everybody.

Pages 7-11 of the handbook suggest several activities that girls can do to help them understand the Girl Scout Law. In addition, there is an example of a situation where the Girl Scout Law might help a girl decide what is the right thing to do. The girls are asked to decide what they would do in this situation, and then to think up some real-life situations of their own for every part of the Girl Scout Law. To do this, they may need some help from you. Here are some additional examples just to give you a head start.

To be honest. You are playing on a team in a game that all of you really want to win. You notice that during the game the scorekeeper gives your team an extra point by mistake. At the end, your team wins by one point. What would you do?

To be fair. Your leader's daughter is a member of the troop. Because her mother is the last one to leave the meeting place, the daughter always cleans up and puts things away. What would you do?

To help where I am needed. Your mother asked you to baby-sit for your sick baby sister while she went to pick up some medicine. You want to watch your favorite television program, but the TV is far from the baby's room. What would you do?

To be cheerful. You had counted on having a certain kind of ice cream at your party. Your mother bought a different kind because the store was out of your favorite. What would you do?

To be friendly and considerate. Your patrol is waiting in line at the grocery store with a lot of food for a camping trip. There is a father with a crying baby behind you, buying just two items. What would you do?

To be a sister to every Girl Scout. Names of buddies have been picked out of a hat for the next activity. You get the name of a girl you don't like. What would you do?

To respect authority. The camp director has told you not to bring radios to summer camp. You have a new transistor radio and you want to show it to your friends. What would you do?

To use resources wisely. Your mother packs a sandwich for you to take on a hike. When you open it, you discover it is smooth peanut butter; you like the crunchy kind. What would you do?

To protect and improve the world around me. Your schoolyard is always a mess. It is full of candy wrappers, soda cans, and other junk. What would you do?

To show respect for self and others. There is a girl in your troop who cannot eat certain things because of her religion. You are planning a menu. Your favorite food is something she does not eat. What would you do?

When girls are making up situations based on real-life experiences, caution them not to describe any girl or adult too personally. Girls could act out the situations they create. Reactions could be shared by the whole group together or in smaller groups or patrols.

Girl Scout Ways

(handbook page 11)

When Girl Scouting is new to girls, help them become familiar with Girl Scout ways. The Girl Scout Promise and Law, sign, quiet sign, friendship circles, motto, slogan, and service all symbolize the nature of Girl Scouting.

Active self-government with adult guidance shows the girls how Girl Scout activities are developed by them and based on their needs.

On page 13 of the handbook, the motto is quoted in ten languages other than English. Seeing the motto in these languages and learning to say some of the words can help girls develop a sense of the international nature of Girl Scouting. To further build their understanding, you could do the following:

> Get a map of the world and help girls locate the member countries of the World Association of Girl Guides and Girl Scouts (WAGGGS). An up-to-date list of these countries appears on the last page in each issue of the *Council Fire* magazine. Ask your council about this. Help girls find out how many of the countries use the various languages listed in the handbook. In which ones is French the official language? Spanish? German? Swahili? And so on. (Don't forget English!) Are there some World Association countries left over? The girls could find out what the official languages are for those countries, too. Perhaps they would like to learn how the motto is said in those countries.

> Your girls might also try to imagine how girls in other Girl Guide and Girl Scout associations interpret their motto. What kinds of things might they do to "be prepared"?

As the handbook points out, doing good turns and carrying out service projects are among the ways that Girl Scouts keep their promise to serve their country and mankind. This kind of activity also helps to satisfy the need to be needed that many children feel. Help the girls to think up good turns and service projects that they would like to do, for a need that they can identify. Usually this will be something they can do for someone at home, or in their school or neighborhood.

Sometimes girls may need to learn something new to help on a service project. For example, if a troop wants to plant trees in their schoolyard, they will first have to learn how.

32

Help the girls to match their skills with useful and needed service, and also to identify and learn new skills that prepare them to be truly helpful.

Often a patch, badge, or sign activity includes or can be combined with service. When the troop learns several songs, they might visit a senior citizens' center to sing for (or with) the senior citizens. If the girls plant seeds or bulbs as a nature project, they could plan to have enough so that some of the little plants could be used to decorate the center.

The Girl Scout Uniform

(handbook page 15)

Wearing a uniform is one of the privileges of being a Girl Scout. The uniform helps the girl to see herself as part of a special group. It also provides a link with other girls around the world who wear the distinctive uniforms of their own Girl Guide or Girl Scout associations.

While girls are encouraged to wear a uniform, it is not required. The membership pins and World Association pin can be worn on regular clothing. However, every effort should be made to help girls get uniforms if they want them but can't afford them. Sometimes councils can help provide uniforms for girls in this situation. And sometimes sponsors offer to help individuals.

The illustrations in the handbook show girls without uniforms in a wide variety of situations because we do not want the girl without a uniform to feel that she is not a Girl Scout in the fullest sense.

Like the girls, adult Girl Scouts are strongly encouraged—though not required—to wear uniforms, especially at troop meetings and official events.

If you do not wear a uniform, you should still wear your Girl Scout pin and World Association pin to troop meetings and other Girl Scout events.

See the *Girl Scout Uniforms, Insignia, and Recognitions* booklet for information on the proper way to wear the uniform and the correct placement of insignia.

How Girl Scouting in the United States Began

(handbook page 20)

The story of Juliette Gordon ("Daisy") Low and the founding of Girl Scouting in the United States is a fascinating one. In the handbook, it is illustrated with a number of photographs to help girls see Daisy as a real person, who once was a young girl like themselves. Some girls will be able to read the story, but others will not. You may want to read it to the whole troop. Also, you might encourage the girls to carry out some of the activities suggested (at the end of this section in the handbook) for following in Daisy's footsteps and for celebrating her birthday.

Girl Scouting's Special Days

(handbook page 29)

Juliette Low's birthday, Thinking Day, and the birthday of Girl Scouting in the United States are traditional Girl Scout "holidays." Note the dates on your calendar so you and the girls don't forget them.

Holidays help foster historical understanding, a spirit of adventure, and a sense of belonging. They also give you and the girls a chance to do some long-term planning.

The handbook suggests a number of activities that girls might carry out in observance of the Girl Scout holidays. These suggestions can always be supplemented by other ideas your girls dream up. A ceremony, a visit by or to another troop, the presence of invited guests—all these can make an occasion special, as can a party or costume atmosphere. Games or skits can be used or adapted from many sections of this book, depending on group interests. You might also check with your council to see if special events have been planned and help girls participate in them.

Ceremonies for Girl Scouts

(handbook page 31)

Ceremonies in Girl Scouting are used to honor special occasions, to recognize accomplishments, or simply to begin or end a meeting. Ceremonies also provide a means of expressing feelings and values of friendship, patriotism, and service. Ceremonies can be formal or informal, with or without guests. They can be held by large or small groups. The people participating in them can stand or sit in a circle or horseshoe, in facing lines, or around a campfire.

A ceremony can be long or short. What it includes is up to the group planning it. Sometimes different groups will plan different parts of a large ceremony.

Girl Scout ceremonies are not required to follow a set procedure but may open, carry out the purpose, and close in a number of ways. The ages of the girls, the season or location, and the purpose of the ceremony will help determine what goes into the ceremony. A troop may build up a repertory of songs and collect a file of poems, readings, and quotations, to be used in ceremonies.

You as the leader will have to give many suggestions and much help with planning in the beginning. When girls have seen and taken part in a few ceremonies—a flag ceremony, an investiture, and so on—they will begin to have ideas of their own.

Work with a committee, a patrol, or the Court of Honor. Explain the purpose of the ceremony and have the girls talk about appropriate behavior during a ceremony. Discuss the form of the ceremony, using questions to help make a plan. Ask:

Where will the ceremony take place?
How will we begin the ceremony?

How will we do the main part?

What songs, poems, quotations should we include?

How will we end the ceremony?

Who will do each part? an individual? a group?

What do we need? candles? decorations?

Who will bring them?

Who will start the songs?

Preparing for Ceremonies

Some ceremonies, such as the opening or closing of a meeting, require preparation only by the persons attending them. The leader of the ceremony can give the quiet sign to get the attention of the troop; then give any direction necessary, asking the troop to sing or take part in other ways.

Other ceremonies require preparation by the troop. The entire troop may need to learn a particular song. Groups and individuals such as a choral reading group, readers, and the color guard must practice their parts. The ceremony may lose its effectiveness, however, if it is rehearsed word for word.

You can help the girls gain confidence by having them walk through the mechanics once or twice. Each girl should know the order of events and exactly what she is to do all the way through. For example:

Will everyone walk in together?

Does she stand or sit during ceremony?

What is the order of events and what part does she follow?

How does the group disperse at the end?

Parts of the ceremony may be announced as it goes along, or the troop may prefer to have one part follow another without announcements. If a girl forgets her cue, or does her part out of order, you can cue in the next part with a few simple words. "Jane will now read a poem on friendship."

Make a final check just before the ceremony to be sure everything is in place and ready to use: pins ready to present, lists of names for insignia presentation, candles and matches ready, campfire laid, fire safety provided for.

Guests at Ceremonies

Occasionally, the troop invites guests to a ceremony. These may be families, troop committee, another troop, program consultants, members of a sponsoring group. Remember, some ceremonies lose their meaning if they become a "show" or performance for an audience. For ceremonies in which girls make or renew their Girl Scout Promise, or when they wish to express deep feelings and aspirations, help them think carefully about the role of guests. If guests attend, help the girls to indicate—by the tone of the invitation and the atmosphere of the ceremony itself—the highly personal nature of the occasion.

If guests are coming, girls should arrange to arrive at least an hour early to arrange the room and make preparation. Be sure some girls are assigned as hostesses and others to cleanup.

You, or one of the girls, can open with a short greeting and an explanation of the purpose of the ceremony. Give guests directions, at the appropriate time, if they are to participate in a flag ceremony. If you use a horseshoe formation, have the open end toward the audience.

As indicated in the handbook, Girl Scouts have some ceremonies that are particularly important. They are investiture, bridging (including fly-up), rededication, Court of Awards, Scouts' Own, candlelight, and flag ceremonies.

Investiture

An investiture ceremony is held when one or more persons join Girl Scouting for the first time. The girl or adult who is being invested makes the Girl Scout Promise, receives the appropriate membership pin (Brownie Girl Scout pin for Brownies, trefoil Girl Scout pin for all others), and is welcomed into Girl Scouting.

Consider whether this would be the best time for girls to receive their World Association pins; there is no set rule.

Here are three sample investitures for Brownies. Use any variation you wish. The first one can also be used for Juniors, with appropriate adaptations in wording, etc.

Troop in circle or horseshoe formation—no special equipment needed.

Ask the girl a simple question: "Why do you want to be a Brownie Girl Scout?" or "What does it mean to make a promise?" The girl answers in her own words.

Ask the girl to make her Promise. Help her if she is shy. Ask: "Do you promise to serve God, your country and mankind...?" This will help her recall the words. As she makes the Promise, she uses the Girl Scout sign and the troop stands quietly.

Pin the Brownie pin over the girl's heart, telling her she is now a Brownie Girl Scout. Give the Girl Scout handshake and welcome her to Girl Scouting.

The girl turns to face the troop and they welcome her with the Girl Scout sign or a song.

Outdoor variation. Lead up to the investiture with any activity you and the girls plan. Have a simple, spontaneous dramatization of the Brownie story. If no brook or pond is available, imagine one.

Take each Brownie-to-be, turn her around, put on her Brownie beanie, and say (or have girl repeat), "Twist me and turn me and show me the elf. I looked in the water and saw _____." The girl looks in the magic pond and sees a Brownie peering up. She says "myself"—and her name.

The girl then tells you she is ready to be a helpful Brownie, stands in the Ring until the others have done the same thing, and waits to be invested.

Enlargement on the simple ceremony for well-established troops welcoming new girls. A "pool" can be constructed in the center of the Brownie Ring by using a mirror edged with greens.

Brownies-to-be are sent outside with the assistant leader. The rest of the troop help construct the "pool."

The troop seats itself around the pool, beside which lie the Brownie pins.

Leader with the Brownies-to-be knocks on the door.

Leader with troop asks: "Who comes to the Brownie pool?"

Brownies-to-be: "We do!"

Leader: "What do you want?"

Brownies-to-be: "We want to be Brownies."

Leader asks why, and girls give their own special reasons.

Girls enter and sit by the pool.

Proceed with ceremony as outlined above.

Investiture for girls joining Girl Scouting at the Junior age level includes the same basic ingredients—making the Girl Scout Promise and receiving the membership pin. Junior troops may want to create their own ceremony for girls who are new to the troop, or if an entire troop is being invested together. Here are some suggestions:

A candlelight investiture often appeals to Juniors. You will find details of a candlelight ceremony on page 36 of the handbook.

After the lighting of candles representing the Promise and Law, the girls to be invested are brought forward to the leader by their patrol leader or other troop members. Each new girl is presented to the leader by a troop member who says: "(Name of girl) wishes to become a Girl Scout."

The leader asks the new girl to make her Promise, helping her if she has difficulty. (The leader may ask each girl a question about what the Promise means to her or what "on my honor" means to her.)

When the Promise is made, the leader pins the trefoil pin on the girl's uniform saying: "This pin tells everyone you are a Girl Scout. I know you will wear it proudly."

After all new members have been invested, the leader or designated girls may say a few additional words of welcome to Girl Scouting and to the troop. The invested girls then return to their places and all the girls renew their promise and sing "Whene'er You Make a Promise."

If all troop members are to be invested at the same time, girls may stay in their places in the horseshoe while the leader moves from one girl to the next. The whole group may say the Promise together when each girl has received her pin and a personal word from the troop leader.

Variation: an outdoor trail investiture. Before the ceremony begins, the trail is marked out by members of the troop who are already Girl Scouts. The girls to be invested are given clues for following the trail (drawings, poems, something related to each part of the Girl Scout Law).

The ceremony begins with all girls to be invested setting out to follow the trail. When they have successfully identified the clues, the trail should lead them to a clearing or some other appropriate setting for the investiture. Here the whole troop gathers to repeat the Girl Scout Promise and Law. Each girl to be invested makes her Promise and receives her pin.

Fly-Up to Junior Girl Scouting

A fly-up ceremony may be planned jointly by the Brownie troop and the Junior troop to which the Brownies are going, or by either of the troops. Ideally, both troops will be present at the ceremony. This is a double ceremony: the fly-up from the Brownie Girl Scout troop, and the rededication to Girl Scouting as each girl renews her Girl Scout Promise and those moving up to Junior Girl Scouting receive their trefoil pin. Usually, both the Brownie and the Junior leaders participate. The essential parts of the fly-up ceremony are:

1 The girl receives Brownie Wings from her Brownie leader.
2 She rededicates herself to Girl Scouting, repeating her Girl Scout Promise and receiving the trefoil pin from the Junior leader.
3 All girls and adults renew their Promise.

An example: Brownie troop and leaders form a ring at one side of the room. Junior troop forms a horseshoe at the other side, with the open end toward the Brownies. The space between may be used to symbolize the transition. (A rustic bridge; a rainbow arch of colored paper strips; stepping stones of cardboard labeled Discoverer, Ready Helper, Friend-Maker; any other prop that the girls may think of.)

Bridging to Cadettes

The ceremony for Juniors who bridge to Cadette Girl Scouting is similar to the fly-up ceremony for Brownies. It is held at the end of the troop year and has many of the same elements. It might include a symbolic bridge and a ceremony of girls crossing the bridge. As part of this ceremony, the Juniors bridging to Cadettes renew their Girl Scout Promise and are welcomed into a Cadette troop. At this time they may also receive the Cadette cockade.

Rededication Ceremony

Girls who have already been invested may wish to have a rededication ceremony, separate from a bridging ceremony, at some time during the troop year. This is a time for them to renew their Promise and review what the Girl Scout Law means to them. It is a time to clarify personal beliefs, values, and commitment. A candlelight ceremony or Scouts' Own is often part of a rededication ceremony.

Court of Awards

This ceremony to present Girl Scout recognitions can be held several times during the year, but not too often.

Time must be allowed for the girls to really achieve something. The first Court of Awards should take place a few months after the beginning of the troop year.

While girls with your help plan the Court of Awards, they will depend on you to arrange for those parts of content that reflect your recognition of and pride in their accomplishments.

Candlelight Ceremony, Scouts' Own, and Flag Ceremony

The "how-to's" for these ceremonies are explained in the handbook, on pages 36-46. Also, see "Festivals of Lights" in The World of People chapter of the handbook.

Note: It is a special honor to be in the color guard of a flag ceremony, so make certain each girl gets a chance to have this honor.

Safety rules should always be considered when planning ceremonies, especially those ceremonies that call for candles or open flames. Consider local fire laws before using open flames at camp or in public buildings. Help girls find safe ways to get the same effects. For example, flashlights, electric candles, or "pretend" candles might be used.

National Centers

(handbook page 47)

For information about Juliette Low's birthplace, write to: Juliette Gordon Low Girl Scout National Center, 11 York Lane East, Savannah, Georgia 31401.

For a folder about Rockwood, write to Rockwood Girl Scout National Center, 11001 MacArthur Boulevard, Potomac, Maryland 20854.

For information about Edith Macy Girl Scout National Center and Girl Scout National Center West, write to the Program Department at National Headquarters (830 Third Avenue, New York, New York 10022).

Brownie Girl Scouting

(handbook page 49)

The section set aside for Brownie Girl Scouts in the handbook, beginning on page 49, is aimed at helping girls recognize Brownie Girl Scouting's adventurous opportunities. Use the handbook to start Brownies thinking about what they can do as individuals and in a troop. These ideas can form the first steps in planning program with Brownies.

The Brownie Story

Beginning Brownies need to know about the Promise and Law before officially becoming Girl Scouts. The Brownie Story can help introduce girls to the concept of helping others, an important element of the Promise and Law.

Read the story aloud, or tell it to girls in your own words. Brownies enjoy acting out this story, often with their own embellishment. They could do this as you read, or older Brownies could put on a play for new girls in the troop.

Troop Government

The Brownie Ring (handbook page 58) is the traditional form of troop government for Brownie Girl Scouts. It is a circle in which each girl shares in planning, in problem solving, and in decision-making with her troop. The girls may form committees to develop plans and carry out decisions. In those smaller groups, each member can have an active responsibility.

As leader, try to help girls speak up about their ideas and take turns expressing their opinions.

Keep Brownie Ring discussions short. Make sure each girl is actively involved. Young girls cannot sit too long, especially if they have just come from school. An active game before Brownie Ring time may help girls "work off steam." If the troop has a snack, they may wish to eat it in the Brownie Ring.

Use pictures, charts, hand-outs, and other concrete materials to increase involvement. Show-and-tell sharing can also liven up planning.

Troop management (planning and deciding, making up the budget for an activity, making rules and assigning jobs, electing short-term officers and committee members) should be carried out in the Brownie Ring.

Sometimes girls will need your guidance in working through ideas until they are accepted by the group. Sometimes a vote is needed to reach agreement.

Using a "dream box" is a good way of responding to each girl's suggestion. Girls will know their ideas are respected even if they are not used immediately. Use a decorated cardboard box (an oatmeal box works well) into which girls can put suggestions in pictures or their own words. Then pull out the ideas when you are looking for new plans. For more about helping girls establish and use the structure of troop government, see the sections on "Girl Scout Ways," "What a Leader Does," and "Getting into Action on Activities" in this leaders' guide.

Hints for Brownie Money Management

Brownie Girl Scouts are too young to understand budgeting on an adult level. However, a strong start can be made through troop financing. Girls of this age certainly know the cost of such things as ice cream cones, soft drinks, and movie tickets. They are capable of deciding whether to spend all their money on a party, to share it with others in a service project, or to save it to buy more troop supplies, such as paints. The troop treasurer can go with the leader to the bank to deposit the troop funds and can report in Brownie Ring on how much money the troop has, and what money is spent for.

Help girls learn to estimate costs of items and to check out their estimates; to shop along with you for supplies and compare prices, amounts, and quality before buying. Help them to see how their own values affect the way they spend their money.

Experience with troop financing can make girls aware that belonging to a troop means more than just attending meetings. It means that each member shares in the expenses; that she gives as well as receives; that, together, a group can do many more things than a girl might be able to do by herself.

As girls grow up, experiences in Girl Scouting can help them grow in their ability to manage money wisely—understanding its value and developing habits of thrift, honesty, and self/reliance.

Managing Brownie Troop Money

Consider troop finances from the standpoint of the girls themselves. Be sure to:

○ Make clear to the girls that some troop activities cost money, while others do not, and talk with them in Brownie Ring about costs in relation to plans.

○ Explain annual membership dues to the girls and to their parents.

○ Be aware of the economic situation of the girls' families. Make certain dues are set at a figure everyone can afford.

○ Discuss troop plans and equipment needs with the parents so that they understand and support them.

Although you handle the troop's bank account, it is their money; you neither add to it from your own personal funds nor remove money without their permission.

Know and adhere to GSUSA standards for money earning (pages 90-91 of this leaders' guide), and your council's standards and policies for troop financing.

Committees

Serving on committees enables girls to take an active part in troop management. After they have decided on a project, the girls can (with your assistance) figure out the jobs that need to be done in order to carry out the project. List these and form a committee for each of the main tasks to be done, perhaps grouping some together.

Committees can be formed by letting girls volunteer for the jobs they wish to do or by a chance method such as drawing from a hat or counting off by number of tasks to be done. Each committee could have a special name or symbol. A kaper chart could be used (see handbook page 34); or girls may suggest other methods.

Routine tasks could be rotated. If they could seem like a game, so much the better. Setting up, moving chairs, and cleaning up are all tasks that Brownies should be responsible for, either in alternating teams or all at once. Some leaders make cleaning up a ceremony or game of Brownie "magic" at the end of the meeting.

Officers

The group can have whatever officers it wants. They might include a president or chairman, a secretary or scribe, and a treasurer. At first, officers are selected by the leader, perhaps through a lottery or by drawing names out of a hat. Each girl should have a chance to be an officer so that she understands, from firsthand experience, what is involved. This may be a girl's first leadership experience.

When the girls agree on the kinds of officers they want to have and understand the jobs each officer will do, voting can take place. Brownies' terms of office should be short, to give others a chance.

Make sure each officer's job is simple and clear to the girls. You may need to help a girl through her job the first few times. Shy girls, especially, will need your support and encouragement.

Brownie Smile Song

The "Brownie Smile Song" (handbook page 61) is a tradition among Brownies. They love to sing it and enjoy acting out the lines.

The Smile song is a good beginning song to teach the troop. The girls may want to sing it at their investiture.

The Brownie B's
(handbook page 62)

The Brownie B's are a unique feature of Brownie Girl Scouting. To the girls, the Brownie B's mean simply: "This what we can be because we are Brownies and because we have a troop and grown-ups to help us."

To you as leader, the B's offer direction in planning with freedom to go where discoveries lead. They offer appealing, girl-tested ways to encourage growth in relation to the goals of the four Program Emphases.

Each of the Worlds offers many activities related to the Brownie B's. Girls should be encouraged to sample activities in all areas so they will be exposed to the full spectrum of Girl Scouting.

The Brownie B's can help girls see a structure in what they are doing and help them decide what to do when planning. The B's also encourage continuity in growth. For example, if a girl is enthusiastic about learning or finding out something (being a discoverer), she could share her knowledge with a friend (be a friend-maker), or use it to help someone else (be a ready helper).

When you introduce the Brownie B's, the girls could talk about what they think each one means and how a girl could be a discoverer, a ready helper, and a friend-maker. The B's are quite flexible. Often a single activity can encompass all three B's.

Discovery activities have a natural appeal for girls of Brownie age. As leader, you can help guide the natural curiosity of children into a constructive effort to discover the how's and why's of the world. Try to provide a rich variety of experiences; Brownies explore widely but not deeply. They switch interests suddenly and often. Pursue Brownie questions and wonderings. Go on quests and discovery trips.

Discovery trips can be as simple as a walk around the block or as ambitious as troop camping. Plan ahead; share ideas about courtesy and safety.

o Discuss plans for the trip in Brownie Ring. Help the girls know what to expect and what will be expected of them.

o Encourage the girls' curiosity as they explore. Have fun! Discover along with them.

o Be honest when you don't know something. Maybe one of the Brownies has an answer or can get one. Maybe you can go back and look it up together or find someone who can supply the information.

o In the Brownie Ring, look back on each trip or experience and discuss with the girls what was best about the experience and what you would do differently the next time.

See the resource list at the end of this book for more discovery ideas.

Ready helper activities reinforce one of the fundamental elements of Girl Scouting—that of giving service. Ready helpers can help at home and school, in their troop, in their community.

o People want to feel needed, regardless of their age. Help girls see that what they do is useful and needed by others.

o Help girls decide on individual and group projects and to gain skills they may need to carry these out.

o Girls may wish to make personal contracts on ways they will help at home.

o Even the youngest girls can try community projects. Help them see firsthand the results of their efforts.

o Encourage girls to explore the meanings, in action, of the Girl Scout motto and slogan.

Friend-maker activities help girls to initiate and maintain friendships, to increase their understanding of themselves and others, and to learn to use basic interpersonal skills. Brownies can also be friends to the environment by taking care of it. See sections on The World of People and The World of the Out-of-Doors, in the handbook and in this leaders' guide, for more activities.

o Create ways for Brownies to use interpersonal skills in their friendships with others.

o Encourage interest in Brownies around the world as a first step in international friendship.

o Use stories, games, songs, festivals, face-to-face experiences, to open girls' eyes to the wonderful variety of The World of People.

o Help girls respect the environment when planning and carrying out their activities.

The official Brownie B patch is a special insignia earned by Brownie troops. Remember it is a recognition for participation in selected troop activities, not for individual achievement. Turn to page 64 of this leaders' guide for basic facts about the patch, and to page 64 for guidance on how to use it.

Activities suggested for the Brownie B patch, on pages 63-67 of the handbook and pages 65-72 of this leaders' guide, may be used as troop activities apart from the patch. Girls may try the patch activities as outlined, or as starting points for their own ideas about the Brownie B's. The number of idea possibilities is unlimited.

Bridging to Junior Girl Scouting

Ideally, every Brownie troop has a Junior "sister troop" that Brownies will join when they fly up. The most meaningful bridging activities involve personal contact between girls in the Brownie bridging group and members of the Junior troop they are to join. If visiting a Junior troop or meeting individual Juniors is impossible, you can still help the Brownies become familiar with Girl Scouting at the Junior age level. You will find suggested bridging activities for Brownies on page 68 of the handbook. Although these activities are linked to the Bridge to Juniors patch, they can be equally useful for girls who are not working on the patch.

For more information on the Bridge to Juniors patch, turn to page 72 of this book. For information about the bridging ceremony, turn to page 34.

The Path of Junior Girl Scouting

The special section for Juniors in the handbook, pages 69-82, reflects the basics of Girl Scout program at the Junior age level. After a brief introduction to the recognitions earned by Juniors, there are detailed explanations of the different ways a Junior troop may choose to govern itself.

For Junior Girl Scouts the handbook is supplemented by a book, *Worlds to Explore: Junior Badges and Signs*, which provides complete information about the purpose and requirements of Junior recognitions and what girls need to do to earn each one.

Girls who move into Junior Girl Scouting from a Brownie troop will be ready to progress

o from self-government in Brownie Ring to a representative form of government

ʊ from participation in Brownie B and Bridge to Juniors activities to earning Junior recognitions.

They will also be familiar with the five Worlds of interest in Girl Scout program.

Girls who first become Girl Scouts at the Junior level may have had no previous experience in self-government, and they will be discovering the five Worlds for the first time. They can, however, be fully participating members of the troop. Don't underestimate the degree of maturity they have gained or the contribution they can make as a result of experiences outside of Girl Scouting.

All girls who enter Junior Girl Scouting should find opportunities to

ʊ govern their own troop

ɔ choose, plan, and develop their own activities with the aid of an adult partner

o explore a wide variety of interests.

The handbook section on "Becoming a Girl Scout" (page 6) contains important information for Juniors who are new to Girl Scouting.

Junior Badges, Aide Patch, and Signs

(handbook page 18)

The *Junior Badges and Signs* book tells girls, "Your leader will help you decide" what badges to earn, how to develop or change requirements, which way to earn a sign. Turn to pages 73-74 of this leaders' guide for specific suggestions.

Troop Government

(handbook page 71)

The handbook suggests three forms of democratic government that a Junior troop could try: the patrol system, the steering committee system, the town meeting system.

The first two are representative as well as democratic forms of government; they are usually best to use with a large group. The third system, town meeting, is useful when the troop is quite small. It is similar to the Brownie Ring, permitting participation by the entire group.

The handbook emphasizes the patrol system, which has been traditional in Girl Scouting because dividing into small groups enables every member to play an active role in the troop's affairs. (The steering committee, while representative, does not ensure as much opportunity for each girl to make her views known.)

A troop may select any of the three systems. After using a system for an agreed-upon period, the girls may want to evaluate how well they are doing with it. Perhaps they will find ways to improve their use of this system, or they might want to try another one. Patrols and committees can also be reorganized to suit the changing needs of the troop.

It takes time, however, to learn to work together in any system; trying something for just a few meetings is not a fair trial. How long a trial is "enough" will depend on how actively the system is used as a tool for self-government, and on how strongly the girls feel about keeping or changing it.

Some questions to ask—and answer—when deciding whether to keep or change a system might be:

ɔ Is it really working for us? Does this system help us to be self-governing? to make decisions that have to be made? to do things we want to do in ways we want to do them?

ɔ Is it comfortable for us? Can we use it with a reasonable amount of effort and time? Is it fun and exciting, or burdensome, confusing? Does it fit our style, the way we like to manage things?

ɔ If we are uncomfortable, is it the system or just problems of time or misunderstanding? Are we sure we know how it's supposed to work? What are the problems as we see them? Might we have similar problems whatever system we used?

ɔ What would make it work better? What would we need to do differently?

ʊ What are the alternatives? How do other systems operate? What do we like and dislike about each?

When girls serve on a steering committee or as patrol leaders in the Court of Honor, they are making decisions that affect the entire troop. They will need to be sure how the girls they represent feel about any decision that is to be made.

Also, in a representative form of government, reporting back is necessary. At whatever level decisions or discussion take place—a steering committee, Court of Honor, patrols—everyone who will be affected should be informed and given the opportunity to express her opinion.

Before deciding on a system of troop government, you might like to try it out. See if you and the girls can think of a pretend project and make a game of carrying it through the whole process of the patrol system (or steering committee or town meeting). In this way the troop can find out how the system really works.

When the patrol system is new to most girls in the troop, small patrols (five or six girls each) are recommended. This gives each girl a chance to be heard and participate. Selection methods can vary (see suggestions on page 72 of the handbook). However, each girl should think the method is fair and understand how and why the choices were made. Be flexible. If a girl is unhappy, respect her feelings and try to work out another arrangement.

Patrols or committees can be used in many ways. Based on interests, different patrols could be working towards different goals. Some could be doing signs while others are doing various badges, and others are doing activities with no signs or badges.

Patrols can be used as work groups for activities that the whole troop does. Each takes responsibility for some part in the total project. This also applies to regular troop meetings where jobs like "game," "clean-up," "set-up," "ceremony," "refreshments" may be divided up.

Whatever governmental system they use, girls will need to consider what rules their troop wants to have. Most rules can be changed as situations change. But health and safety rules should be strictly adhered to at all times. Refer to *Safety-Wise* whenever there is any question in this area.

Leadership roles should be changed often, perhaps two or three times a year, to give all girls a chance to try them.

Help girls to see that there are many opportunities for them to be leaders, whether in the troop government system or in other ways. "Leader" need not be synonymous with "officer."

Planning

Girls of Junior age are ready to start planning with an overall approach. The handbook (pages 77-80) introduces them to basic steps in the planning process. For information about how you as leader can help them learn to plan, see page 19 in this leaders' guide.

Money Management

The money for troop activities comes from troop dues, which girls contribute. The money is theirs. They decide, with your help, on what the dues should be.

Many Juniors receive a small allowance. They have some basic arithmetic skills and can learn how to keep simple books showing the following:

> Money in — from whom
> Money out — why
> Balance to date

Dues collecting and budget balancing may spur an interest in business, banking, etc. Try visiting a bank or a business as a follow-up activity.

Some other suggestions for you:

Keep a close eye on money matters and help the girls when they need it, but let them handle as much as they can.

Make a clear distinction between troop dues and annual membership dues. (See page 12 of this leaders' guide.)

Check with your council for any regulations it may have concerning troop dues and extra money-earning projects.

Remember, this is the girls' money. If the troop has a bank account, follow the recommendations of your council for handling it.

If a girl is unable to pay dues, make sure she is not penalized. Handle any decision with tact so that she is not embarrassed or shamed.

On to Cadette Girl Scouting

Bridging to Cadettes is particularly crucial. By the time girls have finished their final year in Junior Girl Scouting, they are often changing schools and friends. They have many choices of after-school and other social activities. Girl Scouting becomes only one of these choices. It is therefore important to help them learn what Cadette Girl Scouting offers.

Make arrangements for the girls to visit a Cadette troop (preferably the one they might join) so they can see Cadette Girl Scouting in action, talk with the girls about Cadette badges and Challenges, and get acquainted.

This personal contact is very important, especially for the girl who will be going to a new school in the fall. Knowing that she is accepted and that the girls are friendly will reduce her anxiety. Possibly the Cadettes could also help the Juniors begin work on some troop activities. Active membership in Girl Scouting can give a girl the sense of continuity she may need when much within and around her is new and different.

Just as there is a special ceremony for Brownies flying up to Juniors, there is a ceremony for Juniors bridging to Cadettes. For information about this ceremony, turn to page 34 of this leaders' guide.

The Handbook: Five Worlds to Explore

Almost four-fifths of the pages in the handbook are devoted to the five Worlds of program. Here's where girls find the activities that attracted them to Girl Scouting in the first place.

For each of the Worlds, this leaders' guide gives you:

o a description of some ways a girl can learn and grow through her explorations.

o "Suggestions for Leaders," which are tips and ideas for ways to enrich girls' experiences.

o "Index to Activities," which tells you more about some of the things suggested in the handbook; answers some questions that girls might ask; and suggests additional or spin-off activities.

In general, leaders' guide suggestions are keyed to major sections in the girls' book (such as "You're Special" and "How's Your Safety Sense?" in The World of Well-Being). Some of the ideas on The World of the Arts are grouped a bit differently.

The World of Well-Being

Explorations in this World can help a girl to:

better understand her inner self, her values, needs, emotions, and strengths.

develop health and safety awareness in the troop, home, school, community.

be physically fit, to eat properly, care for her body, work, rest, and enjoy leisure time.

build satisfying relationships with others.

make and keep friends, share with family, reach out to others in her community.

Suggestions for Leaders

Many of the activities in The World of Well-Being are aimed at helping the girl see herself as a person of worth. If a girl feels she is not important to anyone, this is a good time to let her know that she is important to you.

Consider well-being. Thinking about oneself and one's values can help contribute to well-being. Things to ponder with girls:

How I feel and act when I'm in a group

What I enjoy doing (and what I dislike)

What parts of Girl Scouting are important to me, and why

What is my body like? How is it changing as I grow older?

Index to Activities

Activities in "You're Special" (handbook page 86) and "How Do You Feel Today?" (pages 88-90 in the handbook) encourage a girl to talk about herself and her emotions. She discovers some of the things that make her special and interesting to others.

An atmosphere of trust and sharing helps people learn about their feelings.

Sometimes girls may be too shy to share. That's O.K. Allow anyone to say "I pass" or "I pass for now." Allow girls to be silent and just listen.

Pretending and acting are used in many of these activities. (See pages 23-24 in this leaders' guide for some techniques.)

In talking and acting out feelings, set limits to protect girls from embarrassment. Girls who have problems in their lives may have difficulty sharing or may need to be limited to give others a chance.

See The World of the Arts for ideas on ways of expressing feelings.

See The World of People for more ideas on helping a girl feel proud of her own heritage.

It is not necessary to have a formal discussion for sharing. Watch for times when girls talk about their feelings naturally, in one-to-one or group conversation.

Sharing feelings when enthusiasm is high, when something went well, when things are bubbling along, can balance the feelings expressed during problem situations or in times of stress.

Handbook pages 91-93 explain how a healthy mind and a healthy body go hand in hand. The concept of balance between activity and relaxation is introduced here.

Help girls relate the information on these pages to their daily lives.

Girls can sit in a circle and talk about such things as how their body feels when they are angry or happy and what their feelings are like when they are sick.

The activity in which girls keep track of what they do could be tried several times during the year, in order to compare.

Handbook page 95 talks about safety in general, with emphasis on the home.

Use *Safety-Wise* as a reference in planning all troop activities.

Safety consciousness can start early. With your help, girls can gain awareness of safety measures needed at specific times and places.

Safety can be talked about in the troop meeting as things happen—or, preferably, before!

Try going through the handbook with the girls, and look for Suzy Safety. Let the girls guess why she's there, and then discuss the situation illustrated or described.

Activities on pages 95-107 of the handbook are based on the importance of play. See page 24 in this leaders' guide for more information on play. Some games in the handbook are for physical activity; others are quiet games for mental stimulation and diversion.

The games in these sections are just a sampling. They could be simplified for younger girls.

Girls may want to keep a record of games played (a "game box" or file) for future reference.

Take the opportunity to discuss being a good sport. Each girl could fill in a chart like the one below.

Sport Scorecard	Could Do Better	O.K.
I play as part of the team		
I try my best		
I practice game skills		
I have fun playing		
I follow game rules		
I play well and enjoy myself even when my side is losing		

In the ideas for games on pages 95-104 of the handbook, the emphasis is on exercise and physical activity.

The "wheel of fitness" exercises could be used for a break when girls are doing quiet activities.

Physical activities are good as starters. After school, children often need to "let loose."

Remember, each girl is at a different developmental level in coordination. Encourage the girls to do their best, but don't push them beyond their natural limits. Vary games so each girl has some opportunities to "star" in what she does particularly well.

Safety tips for bicycling, swimming, and ice skating are included in the girls' book.

Girls enjoy sports, and team sports can be included in the troops' activities. The troop may even wish to play in neighborhood competitions. Check rules from official rule books. Use parents or older Girl Scouts as resources for a sports program. Make sure the girls know and follow the necessary safety precautions.

Games and hobbies suggested on pages 104-108 of the handbook are for times when girls need physical rest. Try these before and after meals, to break up physically active periods, or while traveling.

"Invent A Game" (handbook page 106) stimulates creativity. Children love to make up games for special situations.

Try a wide game. It can be held on any subject in any World or can be a mixture of skills and activities. Wide games (see page 60 of this book) are ideal as an out-of-doors activity, and they are a tradition of Girl Scouting.

Hobbies can lead girls, depending upon their interests, to activities in any one of the Worlds. The hobbies people have tell something special about them. Hobbies help people of all ages enjoy their free time, and may lead to careers. Some hobbies help build skills for daily living. Many girls of Junior age are starting to develop their own hobbies.

Hobbies are a good way to use the skills of parents and others in the community. They might help girls form interest groups or patrols and select badges.

Pages 108-114 of the handbook contain activities centered on the home and general living skills. Much of a young child's life occurs in her home. Where and how she lives, who she lives with, and how they relate to each other all have an effect on the child.

In this section, the uniqueness of each family and way of living is explored.

Help girls to see that, while there may be differences in the way people live, each person's "home place" has special meaning for her. Give them opportunities to talk about their ways of living, their brothers and sisters, parents, guardians, or other adults in their home.

If you want to, share some of your own "growing up" and home experiences with the girls.

Help girls see that everyone in their living environment (including themselves) can make a positive contribution.

The ideas here are things that a young child might be able to do at home. Practice or try some of them at a troop meeting, or do them for a Brownie Ready Helper or Junior badge activity.

Invite parents and guardians or older brothers and sisters to come and talk about what they do during the day, at their jobs, or with hobbies. Perhaps they know something girls would like to learn to do.

"Be a Clever Consumer" (handbook page 112) introduces a basic life skill that girls start learning at home. An imaginary situation, in which girls can try making a consumer decision, is included. You will find that they base their decisions on their own values—what is important to them and how much they know about something. Help link the ideas in this section with troop government and planning. (See pages 18-19 in this leaders' guide for more information on choosing and planning.)

You and the girls might make up and think through other situations, such as buying supplies or planning meals for outings.

Help girls compare cost and ingredients.

Link consumerism to troop budgeting and the problems of time, supplies, and money.

As girls choose among the possibilities, note that Senior girls in the handbook's imaginary situation should be qualified to teach and should know the safety rules.

Pages 114-118 of the handbook are about food and nutrition, and the part they play in overall well-being.

These pages aim to help girls be more selective in what they eat. (Remember that, for those who are overweight or those who have little to eat at home, food may be a sensitive topic.)

The cooking skills listed as "things that are important to know" can be practiced by the troop or a smaller group. They may be part of your preparations for camping, cooking out, or working on a badge.

Girls might learn some of the food-related skills by going on trips to stores or by asking someone to visit a troop meeting and give a demonstration.

The pictures of different people on pages 114-115 of the handbook could lead to discussion of many factors related to food, such as age, weather, physical health, activity, access to food, and background.

Some foods shown in the four food groups, or for "Smart Snacking," will be new to children. How can you persuade girls to sample new food for fun?

The suggested card games could be played and then used for a community service project. Cards could be donated to a community center, or Girl Scouts could use them with younger children as flash cards.

Young girls are interested in babies and younger children. On page 111 of the handbook, they are encouraged to think about their own development from babyhood and about the needs of young children in general.

Consider with girls how a baby grows and how babies act. This may lead to discussion on girls' own growth and development.

If a mother or friend has a young baby, capitalize on this. Invite her to part of a troop meeting with the baby.

This section can be particularly useful to girls who may be asked to watch other children or who will soon be baby-sitting. Talk about safety and some practical rules for baby-sitters.

Another useful skill, sewing, is discussed on pages 119-121 of the handbook.

Bring in supplies from home and talk about the tools of sewing. Invite resource people to demonstrate or to help girls learn.

Base what you do on the girls' ability. Very young girls may be unable to thread small needles and do fine work.

Other things to do: turn something inside out to see how it's made □ visit a fabric store □ look at art that is sewn □ try making simple costumes, doll clothes, decorative items.

The remainder of the handbook chapter on "The World of Well-Being" is devoted to health and safety. Pages 122-124 call attention to community services that girls may take for granted or may know about.

Girls might want to go on a discovery walk or visit the places mentioned.

Find people to visit the meeting and talk about their jobs in health-related fields.

If the girls are interested in how their community works, look at the first few pages of The World of People in the handbook. Explore other aspects of the community, as well as those related to health and safety. (Also see The World of People section in this leaders' guide.)

After a visit, the troop might follow up with a simple service project, letter of thanks, or pictures for a bulletin board.

Being prepared to handle emergency situations is another important aspect of The World of Well-Being.

"Emergency Who's Who," "Fire Safety," and "First Aid" provide the girls with basic information.

For all three topics, discuss why the information is important. Help girls imagine situations in which they might need to know these things, or remember times when emergency preparation was useful.

As a service project, make copies of the basic numbers on the telephone list for others. Leave some blanks for personal numbers. Perhaps the girls would want to include instructions on what to say. They might also enjoy dramatizing how to make phone calls.

Invite a nurse, paramedic, fireman, police officer, or Red Cross aide to talk with the girls about emergencies and first aid; or visit a place where these people work.

Acting out emergencies is a good way to get practice in knowing what to do. You (or girls) could make up situations, call them out (or act them out) and then have girls react. Afterwards, discuss what they did.

Make up emergency and first aid games, such as quiz games or an emergency wide game (for wide games, see page 60 in this guide).

Practice a troop fire drill, both at the meeting place and at camp. If you don't know the procedure, find out.

Follow the first aid instructions in the handbook yourself. For a more complete adult course, consult your council or the local branch of the Red Cross.

Make a first aid kit with the girls, if the troop doesn't have one, and keep it with the troop supplies. Girls could also assemble kits for their homes and family cars as a project.

For Juniors, you should include at least one sanitary napkin in the first aid kit. Let the girls know that it is there and what it's for. Many girls start to menstruate at the age of ten or eleven.

If a girl does start menstruating at a meeting or on a trip, remember that you may need to explain carefully what is happening. Girls can be very upset, particularly if they have not been informed in advance. Reassure the girl that she is not hurt and will not bleed to death. Explain that menstruation is an important sign of growing up—something to be proud of, not embarrassed by.

The World of People

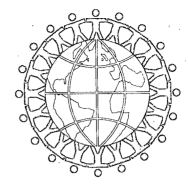

Explorations in this World can help a girl to:

build pride in her heritage, discovering and sharing her own background and family customs, her own cultural experiences.

find out more about her community and the people in it, recognizing the community's needs, the services it offers, and her opportunities to contribute.

see and try out customs and ways of living of others, learning something about the many cultures in her own society and throughout the world, appreciating the uniqueness of each culture and the common themes of all.

sense the oneness and interdependence of all people, growing in awareness of global issues and the basic needs of all people.

Suggestions for Leaders

Recognize the different backgrounds and experiences of girls in the troop. Invite members of their families to talk about special customs or ways of doing things, family history, food, hobbies, jobs, arts.

Help girls develop interest in and concern for others through involvement with people from the many cultures in your community. Be aware of special holidays, celebrations, and concerns of various racial, ethnic, and religious groups.

Personal experience, through visits, trips, guests, is the most effective way of introducing girls to new people, places, roles, and customs.

If you are inviting a guest or going on a visit, find out something about the new friend's culture in advance so that the girls already have some background information. Think of questions to ask, ideas to share, activities to do together.

Need printed resources? Don't forget your school or public library; it often has appropriate books, films, filmstrips, and records. Also ask travel agencies for pictures and brochures.

Index to Activities

This World in the handbook begins (page 133) with activities designed to establish pride by developing an appreciation of the uniqueness and worth of each person's background. Encourage girls to see that there is no "right" and "wrong" way to live, that people in different situations and cultures do different things.

Invite people to visit and share their culture and customs.

As girls watch different people at home and what they do, help them look at the many options they have in their own future roles.

You might invite a senior citizen to talk about what girls (or women) used to do and how things have changed.

Girls can discuss what their mothers and other women in their family do and talk about, and the new things women are doing today.

Girls could discuss what they are now, what they want to be, and what their friends want to be.

Girls could draw, act out, or pantomime the kind of person they want to be and what they would like to do in the future. Help girls to dream of futures that can use all of their human potential.

Pages 136-143 in the handbook introduce the idea of what a community is, and how young girls can contribute to it.

Exploring the history of the community can be treated like a guessing game or treasure hunt. This can lead girls to explore their neighborhood and is a good way of meeting and talking with lots of new people.

These pages can spark trips, visits, and sharing of experiences based on the girls' own interests.

Girls could do collages as well as models or maps; make buildings out of cardboard boxes (and then have a community); make up songs or plays. (See activity suggestions for Brownie B patch in The World of People, pages 68-69 of this leaders' guide.)

Help girls look at the cultures besides their own that are present in the community. Who is in a minority? Is there more than one minority group? What role do they play in the community? Invite different people to talk about these community groups, their contributions, and their problems.

Visit with women at work. Learn what they do and how they do it. Help girls to see women in non-traditional roles.

Look for "hidden heroines" (women who are making special contributions) in your own community. Meet with them, talk to them, to learn about how they started out.

Explore with girls the types of services provided by the federal, state, and local governments. Who makes these services possible? What personal experience have girls had with them? Make a chart and fill it in as girls learn about different services. Here are some possibilities:

Postal Service—mail delivery, stamps, post office.

Defense—Army, Navy, Air Force, Marines, Coast Guard.

Sanitation—garbage collection, snow removal.

Political officials—elected and appointed.

Education—schools, public information.

Consumer and environmental protection—food safety laws, licensing, anti-pollution regulations.

Special services—census, weather.

Agriculture—food growing, research.

Protection—police and fire departments.

Health—public health services, social services.

Transportation—roads, airports, harbors, traffic control.

Justice—court, prisons.

Recreation—parks, playgrounds, libraries, zoos.

With older girls, you might also link these services to citizenship. Find out answers to the following questions:

How are the services paid for?

How are citizens responsible for keeping up community services?

What are the rights and duties of citizens?

How do changes happen in government and elsewhere?

Do all groups in the community receive these services?

The dream community suggested in this World can be used as the starter for many kinds of fun and acting. Make it with big boxes, little boxes, pretend TV screens, any way that you and the girls want. Children could act out the different jobs that people have in their dream place.

Besides the questions in the handbook, girls might consider these things in making their dream communities: population (how many people will there be) and zoning (how to keep it the way girls want it to be).

Talk with town planners, architects, developers. Find out:

about the tools of town planning, such as blueprints and models.

what the plans are for the community you live in.

how decisions about planning are made.

what jobs are involved.

As girls learn about the community, help them recognize not only its good points, but also the needs and problems of the people who live there. Make a list of things that need changing. From this list, girls could look at what they (as individuals, as a troop, or as part of a larger group) could actually do to improve conditions. Make their ideas into a community-action service project.

Suggestions like "Friendship Ideas" (handbook page 143) can be used as service projects. They also make excellent patch, badge, or sign activities. Do these projects based on needs in your community. Base actual activities on the girls' own suggestions as much as possible. Relate these ideas to the "serve mankind" part of the Promise.

Beginning on page 146 of the handbook, the view broadens from a girl's own neighborhood to a much larger variety of places and people. In carrying out these activities, seek out people of diverse cultures who live in your community. They are a great "at home" resource for your troop.

Invite members of several ethnic organizations to share their activities with the girls. Use pictures, films, books, whatever is available.

Some of the friendship activities in the handbook are art projects; others are games, ceremonies, dances, or songs. All are fun. Find more in the Worlds of the Arts and Well-Being, as well as in the section on ceremonies.

Try these activities (or use their products) on days with an international Girl Scout theme, such as Thinking Day or Juliette Low's birthday (see page 45 of this leaders' guide), or on other special occasions.

Activities in the handbook are only samples of what can be done. Girls learn best about another culture through a variety of experiences. Try a group of songs, or a mixture of songs, dances, games, crafts, foods, etc., from one country.

Help the girls to look more closely at familiar games and songs of their own culture. How did they begin? What did the words or actions originally refer to?

There are other types of things to learn about a culture: folk tales, ways of dress, houses, religion, holidays. Girls might also find out about plants, animals, climate, and geography of their family's place of origin.

Many of the activities in this section are done similarly in many cultures. If the girls enjoy Wycinanki (handbook page 154), find out how to do paper designs or cutouts created by the Mexicans, Indians, Scandinavians, Chinese Germans, Swiss, and Pennsylvania Dutch, to name a few.

There are two activities (American Indian and African beadwork) that call for beads. Use any type of beads you like. Find them in five-and-dime stores, craft stores, or toy stores. Beadwork from two parts of the world is included to show that similar techniques are used around the world.

Nearly all cultures use lights for ceremonies at some time. Adapt some of the ideas from festivals of lights in other countries for your next candlelight ceremony. Consult *Safety-Wise* and local safety laws if you want to use real candles.

Have a holiday party. Invite others, and celebrate with the traditions of the girls in the troop, or celebrate with a tradition that no one has tried.

For instructions on making the papier mâché piñata, ask an art teacher, someone from your council, or someone who does it at home.

The "scrambled words" puzzle on breads of the world requires some spelling ability and an acquaintance with geography. If girls find it difficult, they can do it in teams or divide the list. Bring along an atlas or world map to locate the countries of origin.

The answers to the breads of the world puzzle are:

1. Iran	6. Armenia
2. Sweden	7. India
3. Korea	8. American West
4. Belgium	9. Scotland
5. Peru	

(**Note:** Armenia is no longer officially a country. Much of it has been absorbed into Soviet Armenia. Armenians consider themselves to be a "dispersed people," and many now live in the United States.)

Corn cakes are an example of a food girls could make. The girls' book has a traditional Native American (American Indian) recipe. The American Indians introduced corn, which is a native plant, to the early settlers.

Girls might think of other interesting foods to cook. Ask them to bring favorite family recipes for a multicultural potluck meal.

Handbook pages 166-171 highlight interdependency, introducing the idea of global issues.

In general, this section is aimed at making girls aware that (1) people have certain basic needs, which are sometimes not met; (2) sometimes we consume more than we need; and (3) what we do here may have an effect on people in other countries. Be sensitive to girls' family situations. A girl who has little may feel self-conscious or angry about some of these activities. A wealthy girl may feel guilty or overly important.

To make the "Things I Need" list more adventurous, girls can play "Going to Coconut Island."

Imagine you are going on a one-month trip to a faraway island. Coconut Island is big and has nothing but grass and tall coconut trees. You may take four things with you besides what you wear. What will you take?

Girls can then consider the following questions: What would happen if they could bring one friend, or several friends? Would it be easiest alone, with one friend, or with the troop? Why? Questions like these also help girls to examine and clarify their own values—what is more important to them?

Finding out where foods come from can be fun. Read labels, ask the grocer, look in books. Hunt for different foods from various places. This can give girls some basic practice in gathering information.

More to think about: Are any foods grown or processed nearby? Take a visit. Imagine with girls what would happen if there were: a crop failure, a bankruptcy, no delivery trucks or transportation, a strike, bad storms, etc. Think about who would be affected in your community, another town, another part of the United States, or in another part of the world.

The World Food Game, handbook page 169, can be used to understand how much the food supply varies from one country to another. This game works best with older girls, who are better able to imagine the situation and to understand its causes.

e World Food Game questions in a group is
...agine with the girls, as you play, how peo-
...other countries feel.

There are other needs in addition to food. Limited resources such as fuel, water, minerals, forests, and wildlife, in combination with other situations such as pollution and the population explosion, are all global issues. The food game or "needs list" could easily lead to discussions of these issues and surrounding problems. Encourage girls to be aware of such issues—through television, listening to others, observing in their own communities.

Consider with girls what they can do to help people close to home and far away who are affected by these issues.

Local service projects can often help girls be aware of the impact they can have in helping to improve the world. Help them choose simple projects, or join in larger ones, in which they can see results.

There are also many international service projects. Two are listed in the resource section for this World. Check with your Girl Scout council and any other community groups for additional ones.

Sisters Around the World

Membership in the international family of Girl Guides and Girl Scouts can be genuinely meaningful to Brownies and Juniors. In addition to the printed and audiovisual resources listed at the end of this book, there are two special Girl Scout days that offer opportunities for personal involvement:

Juliette Low's Birthday, October 31, is the occasion in many councils for gathering contributions to the Juliette Low World Friendship Fund (JLWFF). If there is a council-

wide event, be sure to find out how your troop can participate. Or your troop can plan its own special event, featuring Daisy's own story (handbook pages 20-28) and some of the songs and games that Girl Guides in other countries enjoy.

Thinking Day, February 22, is celebrated by Girl Guides and Girl Scouts throughout the world. It is the birthday of Lord Baden-Powell, who started the worldwide Guiding and Scouting movement, and also of his wife, Olave, Lady Baden-Powell, for many years the World Chief Guide. On this day, girls think about their sisters around the world and send messages to people they know in other countries. (Brownies or Juniors might know an older girl who was brought to your council with the help of the JLWFF.) Thinking Day is also a time when girls in many places start special action projects or celebrate their completion.

Either or both of these special days could be an occasion for talking about what girls of Brownie or Junior age do to help where they are needed in other countries, and what your troop can do. To take just one example, the picture of Nigerian Brownies gardening (handbook page 171) might start a discussion of hunger as a serious global issue. Each February, the *Leader* magazine brings you fresh news and pictures of Girl Guides and Girl Scouts being helpful.

Let the girls know what happens, in human terms, as a result of their contributions to the JLWFF. This information is highlighted in the *Leader* magazine for February. The World Association of Girl Guides and Girl Scouts has a Thinking Day Fund, used for purposes ranging from disaster relief to helping Girl Guide organizations get started in new countries. Our contributions to this fund are made through the JLWFF.

The World of Today and Tomorrow

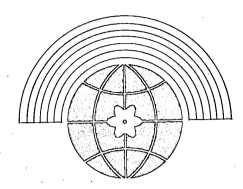

Explorations in this World can help a girl to:

delve into the how's and why's of things that interest her, using her natural curiosity, discovering through problem solving and experimentation, adding to her storehouse of knowledge and skills.

recognize and develop her own creative abilities, combining imagination and skills to meet challenging situations, inventing ways to cope with problems and deal with change.

look ahead to the future, discovering dimensions of growth for herself and her society, seeing the traditional and nontraditional roles of women and men, recognizing ways her present interests can build toward future ones.

Suggestions for Leaders

Exploring, experimenting, and discovering call for a certain amount of risk-taking. Not life-and-limb risk—as a leader you protect girls from such danger—but risk of moving into the unknown, of disappointment, of being embarrassed or feeling silly, of doing things in new and different ways. The discovery way of learning and having fun is not nearly as frightening for girls as it often is for adults. It is young people's natural way of learning—and you can be their partner in it.

If you can help girls to sense their own creative abilities and to develop their ability to question, to find out about and cope with their world, you are helping them feel good about themselves—more at ease with their world, less swamped by it, freer to act in it and affect it.

Know-how is important for some of the things girls will want to do in The World of Today and Tomorrow. But for most girls, learning doesn't depend as much on answers you can supply or subjects you can teach as it does on your awareness of what they want and need to know, your willingness to learn along with them.

Help girls move from the activities suggested in their handbook into more experiments with technical and life skills that interest them.

What makes things work?

What makes people tick?

How do people turn needs and ideas into inventions?

What is a mistake? How have people learned from mistakes? How have you?

Why are people afraid of things?

What kinds of abilities, people, actions do you admire?

Brownie B patches or Junior badges and signs may help girls pinpoint or group subjects they would like to explore.

Include community resource people who can share enthusiasm as well as skills. Look for hobbyists and others—especially women—who can share ideas and information about their jobs, interests, and skills.

Look for special museum or library exhibits and events that are geared to "please touch" discovery.

Index to Activities

The first activity in this World (handbook page 174) encourages girls to learn by exploring ordinary, everyday objects. From the "what happened...?" questions and think-abouts, girls can begin to discover why things do or do not happen under certain conditions. From many separate observations, they distinguish patterns in the way things work.

The girls can explore either individually or as a group. Sharing the discoveries is like a magic show: How was it done? What materials were used? Can I do it? Discovery teams, patrols, other groupings of girls can heighten the adventure of exploration.

Girls can write down this information on charts or draw pictures to show "before" and "after" effects. Keeping a simple record helps girls in planning: What did we do first? second? Where did we go from there? Encourage girls to try to predict what will happen under certain circumstances; then see if their predictions work out.

The questions asked in the handbook can be used as a basic list for exploring other familiar things. More experienced girls can think up other questions to add.

Help girls understand that asking questions is a basic way to look closely at how things work.

A few simple experiments, handbook pages 178-188, are designed to show girls how scientific facts may be discovered through observation and experimentation.

The pages on measuring approach scientific discovery through a familiar activity. At the same time, they introduce a way of doing it that may be unfamiliar to many: the metric system.

For sound educational reasons, the handbook does not encourage converting measurements from traditional to metric, or vice versa. You can do yourself a favor by learning, along with the girls, to "think in centimeters" when you copy and use the ruler on handbook page 176. If you feel too lost without a conversion table, you can find it in many almanacs and cookbooks.

Change to metrics as a way of measuring is a good example of changes that take place in the way people do everyday things.

Explore: What changes have there been in the way people travel, in food preparation methods, in the kind of jobs people (especially women) do? What were these things like in the past? What are they like today? What do girls predict they will be like in the near and far future?

Something more to talk about: How do people react to change? Look at changes girls have experienced in their own lives: a move from one school (or town, or teacher, or troop leader) to another; a new baby in the family; changing from pencil to pen for schoolwork; learning to use a new kind of art material. How did the change make you feel? What did you have to do differently? How did you manage it?

The experiments with water (handbook pages 178-179) are simple enough for young girls to do and enjoy. A commercial "popsicle mold," which many children have, could be substituted for paper cups in the first experiment.

More things to find out about water: How do scientists test water for pollution? What kinds of things pollute rivers, streams, oceans? What can people do to make water cleaner and safer? What are some ways to purify water for drinking? (Also, try the experiment with salt in The World of the Out-of-Doors.)

The "rocket ship" effect with a balloon (handbook page 180) is something that children have done accidentally many times. Now they can find out why it happens.

If the girls want to find out more about space travel, a trip to a science museum or planetarium might be just the thing. Call first to find out what the museum offers in the way of space exhibits for children.

Experiment with principles of flight. Make and fly paper airplanes or kites. Older girls may want to try airplane model kits or to design the "ideal spacecraft" to take the whole troop on a voyage in outer space. (Also see "Worlds Beyond Ours," handbook page 319.)

Make up skits or stories about space, space exploration, life on other planets. (See pages 53-56 of this leaders' guide for ideas on dramatics and creative writing.)

Play a game: how would you communicate with someone from another planet? (The handbook has Morse Code on page 330, ideas for communication without words in The World of the Arts.) What would you want someone from another planet to know about you? (This gets at values and views of self.) What would you want to know about life on a strange planet? What questions would you ask to find out what you want to know?

Explore: What are some of the languages Earth people use to communicate with one another? Learn some phrases in another language.

The experiment on sound (handbook page 181) offers girls a chance to make simple musical instruments and find out what makes them work.

Explore: How do people depend on sound to communicate with one another? What kinds of sounds are happy, scary, and so on? What happens when people cannot hear sound? How do they understand people who speak to them? How do they speak to one another?

Watch a TV show without the sound. Can you understand what is going on? How?

Make music with homemade instruments. Everyone can join in.

Girls might be interested in musical instruments developed by people in other cultures. Can you borrow some from girls' families or from a music teacher? Or perhaps you could go to see them in a museum.

The food activities (handbook pages 181-184) can lead to additional discoveries. What makes dough rise? Have a pretzel experiment. Make doughnuts. See if you can find someone to bring or lend an inexpensive microscope to help girls with the concept of "microorganisms."

The "control" group concept in scientific experiments can be introduced in cooking. Leave out the yeast in one small batch of dough. What happens if you don't knead one batch of dough? Girls can observe the results and note the differences.

Cook indoors or out. Practice measuring and combining ingredients to make foods girls enjoy.

Explore: How does heat change things? Make them better to eat (or, if burned, worse)? See The World of the Out-of-Doors for outdoor cooking ideas. Why does a fire burn? What makes it go out? Talk about safety and first aid measures if clothing or food catches fire.

Have a food ingredients hunt: read labels and look for various things that packaged foods contain. Check on family kitchen shelves and in supermarkets for these ingredients. Why are some good for your body and others harmful?

Magnets (handbook page 184) are fun to use and can form the basis for explaining the workings of a compass. Identify some uses of magnets that are not listed in the handbook.

In the experiments with light (handbook pages 186-188), girls start with the familiar (a rainbow) to discover light waves (what else is a wave?) and reflected light.

"Make a Pinhole Camera" (handbook page 189) is a practical experiment to find out how light produces a picture on a film. Girls may be interested in the different models of cameras, especially the evolution of the "instant" picture. Encourage picture-taking at troop meetings and special events. Share photographs from home. How were they taken? Look at subjects, lighting, camera use.

Further interest by girls could lead to a study of the development of the motion picture as a natural offshoot of still pictures.

Clues to further activities: How is light used at home, in school, in the troop meeting place? in medicine? in industry and communications? What is a good light for reading? Have you ever had an X ray? How does an X ray work? How is it used? How is your eye lens like a camera lens? In TV shows about space and the future, how is light used?

"Building It Yourself...An Introduction to Carpentry" (handbook page 194) offers girls the opportunity to use their hands in what, for women and girls, has been an untraditional activity.

With your guidance, girls can explore uses of common tools found in the home, school, and community.

The step-by-step approach is useful to help girls learn to deal with a project from beginning to end—in this case, making something out of wood. The process can be transferred to other things that require planning, problem solving, and making decisions.

When they work with wood, nails, finishes, and paints, safety considerations should be discussed beforehand with the girls. Examples are proper ventilation before painting; why lead-based paints should not be used for children's furniture; why it is important to read labels and instructions for tools, paints, etc. What-to-do-if's (a finger is punctured with a nail; glue gets into a girl's eye) are important to discuss ahead of time. Stress avoiding accidents through safe ways of working and using tools.

Get helpers (women, men, older Girl Scouts) when the girls plan to do a big job. Newspapers, smocks, old clothes help make the task easier because girls don't have to worry about messes.

Pages 201-205 of the handbook focus on inventions: useful things that people create to make work easier.

Girls can play guessing games, adding their own ideas to the "disguised tools and machines" list. Some Juniors might like to make crossword puzzles using the names of machines and other items used around the house.

Suggest that girls choose, from among various tools and equipment, the things they want to learn how to use. Some they could try out at troop meetings (e.g., typewriter, record player, screwdriver, needle threader, stapler); others they could try in their own home (e.g., stove, sewing machine, fan, washing machine, hand drill) or on a visit to someone who can demonstrate and teach how to use them.

To get started on the invention game, brainstorming is a good technique to use. Page 23 in this book tells you how to do it.

Try brainstorming with everyday items. "How many different ways can you think of to use (salt shaker, shoe, alarm clock, paper cups, etc.)?" Invite girls to suggest new ways to use familiar things.

To play the invention game described in the handbook, encourage girls to use many ways to develop, describe, and compare their inventions: drawing, three-dimensional models and constructions, written lists and descriptions, demonstrations and talks.

For Junior Girl Scouts: see Sign of the Arrow, "Making Things Happen," and Sign of the Star, "Communications," in *Worlds to Explore: Junior Badges and Signs*, for activities related to inventing and creating.

Thought starters: What are some of the useful inventions of past and recent times? Who were their inventors? What makes a person want to invent something? Are there any inventors living near you? Look for men, women, and children who have invented something for everyday use.

Some girls in the United States have had inventions patented. Find out how this is done.

The remainder of the handbook chapter on The World of Today and Tomorrow (pages 206-209) suggests activities to help girls become aware of the many choices open to them. Some possibilities are listed so that girls have a point of departure.

If your troop plays the game of "Who Says So?" (handbook page 206) be sure to use many different kinds of magazines: sports and camping publications, news and gossip magazines, as well as women's and children's periodicals and Girl Scout magazines.

Looking to the world of the future, girls are advised to think about the kind of job they would like, and to visit people at work. Parents, friends, and other people in the community can suggest jobs that might not readily come to mind. If girls visit workers or invite someone to come and tell about a job, help them make up some questions ahead of time to ask these people. Base the question list on what the girls really want to know.

The local library may have a civil service list and other job postings on its community bulletin board; these may expand a girl's job interests.

Remember: Girls are only making career explorations, not career choices. Don't try to go beyond what they are interested in knowing. Support them in feeling that they are participating fully in life right now, at home and in the school community. Each person has value for what she is as well as for what she may become.

The World of the Arts

Explorations in this World can help a girl to:

enjoy, developing a personal taste and appreciation for the many art forms and things of beauty in the world around her.

express herself, using the varied language of art to communicate her own thoughts, feelings, ideas, and ideals.

create, combining thought, imagination, art medium, and skill in her own unique ways.

Suggestions for Leaders

Art is a way of describing and expressing feelings. Use art frequently in combination with activities in any of the other Worlds of interest.

You don't have to be an expert to guide young girls in their arts explorations. Use your imagination, and encourage girls to use theirs. Look for people who have interests, talents, and skills to share with the troop. Invite these people to visit. Visit them. Try things for yourself.

Consider the girls' experience when planning with them for art activities:

Find out what they already know about visual arts, crafts, music, drama, dance, reading, writing.

What arts experiences have they had in school? at home? in Girl Scouts? other places?

Have they visited museums? looked in art books? gone to the library? been to plays or concerts?

Do they play a musical instrument? Have they acted in school or neighborhood plays?

Find out what they are doing this year in school, and what they enjoyed (or didn't enjoy) last year. Together, you and the girls can plan ways to supplement these experiences.

Note that many of the measurements in this World are in metric units. See page 176 of the handbook for a metric ruler you can copy.

Even among girls of the same age, abilities can vary significantly. Help the girls choose the activities that will bring enjoyment and satisfaction to each one.

Some young girls will have trouble with fine detail and delicate tools. Help them enjoy their own stage of physical development by finding satisfying projects that call for large movements and easy tools.

Some arts skills require practice and patience, some projects take longer than others to complete. When you plan with girls, help them remember to set aside time at several meetings if they are doing a large project.

Appreciation for the talent, skill, and patience of others often arises from one's own struggles and mistakes in trying to accomplish something. Help girls to take pride in what they are able to do and to respect the experience and skill of other artists.

To all arts, girls bring their own dexterity, way of seeing, and personal feelings. In most art forms, there is no "good" or "bad" way to create.

As girls get older, they often become self-conscious about art. You are in a position to encourage creativity without fear of grades or harsh judgments.

At best, time for arts is limited in most troops. Make every experience a meaningful one.

Avoid rigid patterns, imitations, mass production (everything alike).

Encourage activities that offer each girl an opportunity to express herself creatively, develop taste and appreciation, learn skills that can lead to lasting interests and vocations.

Above all, make sure that any art is the girl's own creation. If she is happy about it, she will try again.

Examples of Visual Arts

The arts chapter of the handbook contains many examples of fine art and folk art, selected to illustrate techniques and visual qualities discussed in the text. These examples are not intended as a survey of art history; however, they are identified in this leaders' guide so that you can help girls to find out more about the ones that especially interest them.

Handbook page	Title and Medium	Artist
213	Navajo Boy Sand Painting, silkscreen	Harrison Begay, American (Navajo Indian)
213	Sunday Afternoon, watercolor	Adolf Dehn, American
213	Little Dancer of Fourteen Years, bronze	Edgar Degas, French
219	The Music Room, etching	James McNeill Whistler, American
221	Sky Cathedral, wood	Louise Nevelson, American
223	The Whale Ship, oil	Joseph Turner, English
224	Portrait of a Young Girl, oil	Mary Cassatt, American
224	In the Meadow, oil	Pierre Auguste Renoir, French
224	Bridge over Pond Lilies, oil	Claude Monet, French
224	Woman with Chrysanthemums, oil	Edgar Degas, French
236	Young Artist at Work, woodcut	Irving Amen, American
285	Water of Flowery Mill, oil	Arshile Gorky, American

Handbook page	Description and Material	Origin
214	Tribal mask, polychrome wood	Cameroon, late 19th century
214	Scroll: Acrobats, ink and watercolor on paper	Japan, U Kujo-e School, late 18th to 19th century
215	Stained glass, Flight to Egypt	Flemish, early 16th century
215	Pendant, gold	Colombia, pre-Columbian
216	Doll, paper and wood	Japan
216	Basket, split hickory	United States (North Carolina)
216	Tiger, papier mâché	Japan
216	Container, carved and burned gourd	Peru
216	Dolls, painted bamboo	India
216	Bear, carved soapstone	Canada (Eskimo)
217	Ladle, carved gourd	Nigeria
217	Cross, carved wood	Sweden
217	Doll, birch, carved and painted	Japan
217	Quails, carved walnut	United States (West Virginia)
217	Doll, dancer of "false face society," cornhusk	United States (American Indian, Iroquois)
217	Houses, carved tree root	Mexico
220	Stencil for fabric	Japan, Tokugawa Period, 1615-1867
220	Woodcut from Book of Trades	German, 16th century

The carpet on page 247 of the handbook was embroidered in the 19th century by Zeruah Higley Guernsey Caswell of Vermont.

In addition to the pieces itemized above, the chapter is illustrated with children's art representative of work done by 6- to 11-year-olds. The selection includes drawings, prints, paintings, and objects made of clay and plaster.

You can find an endless variety of art works in art history books and museums. Let girls express their own opinions about art, and don't be surprised if their point of view changes as they develop.

Index to Activities

Start with "Arts and You," at the end of the handbook chapter of The World of the Arts. Yes, that's right: the end.

The final paragraph (handbook page 285) can give you an overall look at what this World can offer Brownie and Junior Girl Scouts and a picture of what the girls' own expectations of Girl Scout activities in the arts might be.

Then go to the first few pages of the chapter. Activities on pages 212-215 of the handbook are designed to lead girls into seeing and feeling elements of art in the world around them, the beauty of nature, and of things that people have made. There are activities, too, that encourage girls to feel and to express their feelings through the language of art.

Using the handbook as a guide, help girls recognize rhythm, line, shape, texture, color, and space in everyday things. Note how each child responds differently. Some will be mostly concerned with color, others with texture. Recognizing these elements will give them greater sensitivity in appreciating their own art as well as that of others.

It is in doing, however, that art becomes real for this age group. Girls can begin to see art as communication, not just activity.

The activities suggested on these introductory pages are not meant to stand on their own. They could become part of several kinds of troop activity; try them while traveling, or when you have reached a destination, or after going out-of-doors.

Activities in The World of the Arts

Because the handbook contains such a wealth of suggestions for activities in the arts, tips for helping girls to explore these activities and suggestions for additional activities are grouped below in broad categories. Look for specific art forms (painting, poetry, singing, and so on) in the index of the handbook.

Tips for Doing Visual Arts Projects

Before you start, make a list of the materials that will be needed. Girls can decide which can be borrowed or brought from home.

Be sure everyone knows who is going to bring which item. Work together on getting things organized for easy transport, use, and storage of materials.

Collect! Keep a few basic supplies, such as paint, brushes, scissors, glue, drawing paper, needles, thread, embroidery hoops. From time to time, girls can bring in items for a scrap box—interesting paper, fabrics, ribbons, buttons, and yarns (which should be stored in small balls, sorted by colors, in plastic bags).

Keep plastic, paper towels, and newspapers handy in a troop box, so that you can spread out and clean up quickly.

Remember to leave time for cleaning up. Clean-up should include putting materials back into their box in order, so that they are ready for use the next time.

Two-Dimensional Art: Additional Activity Suggestions

Painting. Finger painting, drawing with chalk, pastels, felt markers, crayons, pencils. Combine crayon and black paint or India ink (this technique is known as crayon resist or crayon etching).

Photography. Make film with home movie camera, develop pictures, make a scrapbook or a slide show. Think how photos might be used in a service project. (How about taking pictures of badly littered spots, for a beginning?)

Collage. Make greeting cards, posters, invitations. Try see-through collage using transparent contact paper.

Prints. Spatter prints, sun prints, rubbings, woodblock prints, linoleum block prints, stencils.

Mosaics. Use bits of colored paper before trying a mosaic with tile.

Three-Dimensional Art: Additional Activity Suggestions

Sculpture. Assemblages are sculptures made from found materials; they can be done anywhere. Carve pine or balsa wood (see The World of the Out-of-Doors in the handbook for jackknife instructions).

Mobiles. Mobiles are a kind of art that hangs and moves. Experiment with papers or shells and other natural materials, indoors and out. Make stabiles; a stabile sits and balances on something, instead of hanging.

Architecture. Look for buildings that don't seem to fit the community; talk about why girls think they are ugly or funny-looking. (This might lead to planning a dream community; see handbook page 142.) Follow a building project from beginning to end. Design a miniature house and make it of cardboard or wood.

Art with Fabric and Thread: Additional Activity Suggestions

Weaving. Try spinning and dyeing the yarn yourselves. Experiment with basketry, another form of weaving. Try finger weaving and various kinds of looms (T-D looms, inkle looms, table looms).

Stitchery. Encourage girls to use stitches as if they were paint, creating spontaneous, free designs. The correctness of a stitch is not as important as the idea being expressed. Try a variety of stitches: blanket stitch, cross stitch, couching, French knots. Try other forms of needlework, such as applique and quilting. Decorate stuffed animals.

Tips for Doing Dramatics

Young children especially love creative dramatics in which they can use their imaginations while being physically active.

Dramatics can range from skits or pantomime to a full play. The key to enjoyment is to start simple and let girls do the designing.

Puppetry may be a good way for shy or self-conscious girls to communicate. They can even do puppet shows with dolls or other toys.

Use dramatics for ceremonies and presentations. Try pantomiming a poem or story while someone reads.

Many schools and community organizations have video equipment and people who know how to use it. They may be able to provide an opportunity for the troop to create a videotape, or just to act out things before the camera. Try to give girls a chance to operate the camera and direct the action.

Watch for live performances, either amateur or professional, that girls would like to see. You may be able to get a group discount on tickets.

Other possibilities for dramatics: charades, shadow puppets, visiting a play rehearsal, touring a backstage area.

Putting on a full play is likely to be a rare and special event for Brownies and Juniors. Much planning, preparation, and time is involved. Forming committees is usually the best way to go about it; in a Junior troop, the committees might be patrols, or special interest groups formed for this project. The following chart shows how jobs might be divided.

Dramatic productions use the talents of many people. Music, art, acting, designing, writing, and planning talents are all combined to make a success on the stage and behind the scenes.

	Before	During
Directing Committee	Write or find a play to produce. Give out copies of script. Hold tryouts for parts (called auditioning). Select people for parts (called casting). Schedule and direct rehearsals, including one complete with costumes and props (called dress rehearsal).	Make sure everything is ready to go. Watch the performance, checking cues, lines, movement, timing, and props.
Business Committee	Decide where production will be staged. Find out how many people room can hold. Make a program to hand out at the performance. Organize publicity—posters, stories for newspapers (town, school, Girl Scout council). Write invitations or sell tickets, collect money, keep records.	Sell tickets at door. Usher audience to seats and hand out programs. Serve or sell refreshments at intermission.
Scenery, Props, and Lighting Committee	Decide on the scenery and props necessary. Design, make, and paint backgrounds. Find and gather props (furniture, small items such as the sticks and moss needed in the Brownie Story). Decide on lighting, if any. Rehearse backstage operations with cast.	Open and close stage curtain. Change scenery and props between scenes. Take care of lighting.
Music and Sound Effects Committee	Collect records or arrange for people to play instruments. Practice sound effects and music at rehearsals.	Provide background music while audience is arriving and during intermissions. Provide music and sound effects during production.
Costume and Makeup Committee	Find clothing to serve as costumes or make simple costumes. Label costumes for each character. Help characters dress at rehearsals. Store costumes.	Put makeup on characters. Have costumes ready. Help characters dress before and during scene changes.
Actresses and Actors	Try out or audition for part. Study and learn parts. Rehearse with cast. Get into costume and makeup.	Make costume changes, if any, between scenes.

Tips on Music and Dancing

If you have been to a councilwide event or a Girl Scout national convention, you know that singing is one of the things Girl Scouts do best. Look in your Girl Scout publications catalog for songbooks suited to girls of different ages and at different levels of musical development.

Girls love teaching their favorite songs and learning new ones. Find out where each new song comes from and what it means. Begin with simple melody lines, then try rounds and canons. Gradually work up to two- and three-part songs or spontaneous harmonizing.

Encourage girls to keep a notebook of the words to songs they like so they can sing them again and again. Repeat newly learned songs so that everyone will remember them.

Remember that the copyright laws do not permit you to reproduce other people's songs without permission.

If you don't feel confident about leading musical activities, there may be girls in the troop who can help you. Older Girl Scouts often welcome the chance to teach songs to younger girls; another Girl Scout adult might help you; or you may know someone outside of Girl Scouting who simply loves to sing.

Find out the types of music and dance the girls are familiar with and enjoy doing. If they are interested only in popular music and dancing, do these by all means; but you could also play classical music softly during quiet activities or combine it with drama, dance, or puppetry. Girls may enjoy discovering music with spoken narration (such as *Peter and the Wolf*) or story music like the *Peer Gynt Suite* or *The Sorcerer's Apprentice*.

Musical activities can begin simply, with girls using their voices, beating rhythm, stamping their feet, or dancing. No special instruments are required for these activities.

Music can be related to almost anything the troop is doing. For example, if you have been stargazing, the music you could listen to and think about ranges from *The Planets*, with full symphony orchestra, to "Twinkle, twinkle..."

In addition to making the instruments suggested in their handbook, girls can find other simple instruments that do not require extensive musical background. Some possibilities are the shepherd's pipe, recorder, tonette, bell, autoharp, and drum.

Do some of the girls already play an instrument? They could make a musical group for a special occasion. If you play an instrument, bring it and join in.

Singing games and folk dances with simple calls and movements are great fun for all. Dancing is something that people of all ages, including brothers, sisters, parents, grandparents, and friends, can enjoy doing together.

If girls want to learn the dances that teenagers are doing, recruit older Girl Scouts, brothers, or someone from a nearby youth center to give lessons.

Attend local folk festivals, amateur ballet, or modern dance concerts; then try some of the movements yourselves.

Tips on Activities in the Literary Arts

Storytelling is as old as humanity. People told stories long before printing was invented. Take time to tell stories of fact and fiction at troop meetings.

Making up a chain story is a fun way to begin. Each person tells a part of the story and passes to the next person, who tells a bit more. Pass a "talking stick" or unwind a ball of string made up of pieces in various lengths. The next person begins when she is handed the stick or when the length of string runs out.

Approach reading as something enjoyable. The children's librarian at your public library can help you make selections appropriate to the ages of girls in the troop. Encourage girls to use books as part of their activities—searching for game ideas, looking up information, reading directions for recipes or trips. Read for excitement and adventure. Read poetry around a campfire. Read to discover things about yourselves and other people.

Girls can write poems, stories, jokes, riddles, mottos, plays. Give them freedom to express their ideas and feelings in their own way. Don't worry if the language or spelling is not correct. Correctness can come later, if the girl wants to put her work into permanent form for others to enjoy.

Combine various kinds of writing with "A Book You Can Make" (handbook page 282). Girls can make books of their original writings to keep or give as gifts.

Have fun with words and sounds. Make up word codes; play word games together. Try to find new words for familiar thoughts and sayings.

Girls who don't write can dictate their stories to someone else or use a tape recorder.

If someone is short of ideas, you might get her started with "Is There a Dragon in Your Backyard?" (handbook page 290, in The World of the Out-of-Doors).

"The Joy of Books" (handbook page 276) challenges girls to find excitement and adventure through reading.

Visit a print shop to see how a book, a neighborhood newspaper, a circular or political flyer is printed.

Make personal bookmarks or bookplates ("This book belongs to _____" or "From the library of _____"). Cover books to protect them.

Read from favorite books in Brownie Ring or in troop or patrol meetings as a way of opening or closing meetings or as an activity by itself. Do a book roundup, as suggested in the handbook.

If you love a poem or book that girls might enjoy, mention it to them when a related subject comes up or read some of it to them in a quiet moment.

Check to see if your public library has a Girl Scout reading shelf. If so, encourage girls to use it and add to it. If not, the troop might like to start one.

Girls might want to read stories to younger children or have a storytelling time at a library, school, or day care center.

Page 278 in the handbook suggests ideas for writing news articles about troop activities, doings of family and friends, and community events, needs, and problems. This can be done individually, in pairs, or in teams, and it can be done outside of troop meetings.

Look at local newspapers to see how news stories are written.

Look at the same news story in a newspaper and on TV. How do the treatments differ? What do you think are the reasons?

Encourage girls to take small notebooks, or several pieces of paper stapled together at the top, on walks, visits, and outdoor activities, and to write stories or draw pictures about the experience. Do this yourself, and exchange notebooks with several girls.

Girls' writings can be used in troop scrapbooks, notebooks, bulletins, and letters to parents or friends of the troop (with their permission, of course).

Combine writings with photography or other visual arts to make displays and exhibits for troop meetings, special Girl Scout events, or public places in the community.

Pages 279-281 in the handbook introduce several kinds of poetic expression to stimulate writing and enjoyment of poetry.

Read poems aloud from the handbook at troop meetings. Bring in others, and suggest that girls hunt for funny poems, sad poems, happy poems, poems that describe scenes, objects, or people.

Try writing poems at a troop meeting, perhaps about what happened on a recent trip or on the way to and from a meeting.

Make up poetry to use in ceremonies. Read other poems written for similar occasions.

The World of the Out-of-Doors

Explorations in this world can help a girl to:

enjoy and appreciate her natural environment, walking, looking, listening, feeling, increasing her awareness of the natural living space around her and seeing herself as part of it.

develop skills and knowledge for living comfortably in her environment, learning and using techniques for adventurous, safe outdoor living while respecting the balance of nature.

take action to protect and preserve her environment, discovering ways to prevent or overcome some of the things that threaten to spoil it.

Suggestions for Leaders

Program in the out-of-doors can provide endless action possibilities for girls and leaders with open eyes and ears and inquiring minds. Activities from all of the Worlds can happen outdoors: you can paint a sunset, run a relay, experiment with a magnifying glass, cook dishes from many cultures over a campfire.

Going outdoors at meeting time is fun for girls and can be a needed release if they have been inside much of the day. Don't be afraid of weather or of going out in the different seasons. Be prepared to modify plans, cover up, wrap up, and have an adventure!

Have something up your sleeve—a compass, a magnifying glass, a piece of rope—to start the girls toward new interests or expand on older ones.

If you have little experience with outdoor activities, join in the wonder and excitement. Find someone who is familiar with the out-of-doors. A senior citizen, a high school student, an older Girl Scout, or a Boy Scout might volunteer to help.

With the girls, find a special troop spot for doing things out-of-doors: perhaps a certain playground, lot, or corner of a park. This makes it easier to make spur-of-the-moment decisions to go out (and families of the girls will know where to find you).

	What to Do	Getting Yourself Ready	Getting the Troop Ready
Step 1	Take the troop outside the meeting place: For an activity in which girls explore the environment with their five senses.	Look around outside. See what exists to help girls learn about the environment, pollution, kinds of buildings, kinds of living things (birds, insects, trees, small plants).	Divide into groups or partners. Describe the kinds of things the group will be doing. Set a time limit, and arrange a signal for return. Define the area in which to stay.
Step 2	Use the troop meeting time for a short expedition to an interesting place not far away: a vacant lot, a park or wooded area, someone's backyard, a brook.	Find what is within a ten-minute walk from the meeting place. Plan how to reach the place safely—crossing streets, and so on. (Will you need first aid equipment?) Arrange for permission from parents or guardians, if needed. Have some suggestions for girls about fun things to do at the outdoor site.	Divide in groups. Discuss and agree on safety precautions and courtesy to the public. Plan something on the way that is fun—like laying a trail, observation games, hiking songs. Together, plan what will happen when you get there. Agree on a time and method of assembling to return to meeting place.
Step 3	Have an outdoor experience nearby for longer than the troop meeting time. Include food that does not require cooking.	Cover readiness for Steps 1 and 2 and: Decide whether hike food is to be a meal or a snack. If a meal is planned, think what makes an adequate meal to bring in a paper sack; a nourishing sandwich, dessert, fruit or raw vegetable, a drink; nothing that requires refrigeration.	In addition to things for a short expedition: Give girls help in deciding what food to bring and what not to bring and why. Discuss and decide whether to bring something to drink, what kind of drink and container would be appropriate. Plan on appropriate shoes, other clothing.
Step 4	Spend a morning or afternoon at an outdoor place with or without a snack or meal that does not require cooking.	Cover readiness for Steps 1, 2, and 3 and in addition: Find out about available toilet facilities and safe drinking water.	Plan where and what time to meet to go and return. Plan what to do: Practice skills for a future outdoor activity: a hike or first cookout? explore? do an outdoor good turn? Plan what to bring and who will bring each thing. Cover troop readiness under Steps 1, 2, and 3.

During any outdoor activity, be sure someone knows where the troop is and when it will be back. And don't forget to talk it over afterwards. Was it fun? What did you see? feel? hear? discover? What should the next adventure be?

Going outside may lead to interest in spending more time out-of-doors, such as hiking or camping. If so, turn to page 59 in this leaders' guide for the next four steps in outdoor activity.

Index to Activities

"Start Where You Are," handbook page 288, is designed to activate the girls' senses as they start exploring their environment.

These activities do not need advance preparation. Girls can use them during a meeting, or as part of a longer outside adventure.

Each activity is a model for many different variations girls can try. For instance, take a magnifying glass and look at a postage stamp size piece of garden; or look at a square of pavement, or a whole block.

Help girls see that there are many ways of using the senses to learn about something. Try these exercises yourself, along with the girls. (Also see handbook pages 212-215 in The World of the Arts chapter.)

"Is There A Dragon In Your Backyard?" (handbook page 290) is a game of observing and describing; both are important skills for enjoying the out-of-doors. Girls find extra pleasure in nature discoveries when they are able to share these discoveries with others. Expressing personal feelings is part of the game, too; listen to what girls have to say about this.

Page 292 of the handbook suggests that girls keep notes or records of their discoveries.

By keeping notes or remembering with pictures, poetry, or tapes, the girls will become more aware of their observations and learnings. School-like notebooks are not the idea here; rather, encourage girls to have a system for remembering what they see.

You might help the girls develop one main notebook or a nature scrap box. (Also see "Literary Arts," page 55-56 of this leaders' guide, for ideas on note-keeping, notebooks, scrapbooks.)

The activities in "Your Environment," handbook page 293, are designed to encourage girls to look more closely at some of the things that share their living space.

Help girls consider the effect that their choices will have on the environment. For example, encourage girls, when buying drinks, to consider the containers they come in, as well as nutrition and taste. They should look closely at all of the facts and then make a decision based on them. For example:

Paper eventually breaks down and becomes part of the soil; is made from trees (a renewable resource).

Plastic does not break down over any time period; made from petroleum (a non-renewable resource).

Glass and aluminum last very long (thousands of years) and require much energy to make, but can be recycled.

Tin and steel rust; cans can be flattened and recycled (made from limited resource).

Link the concept of ecology to The World of Well-Being. Other animals, and the earth itself, need certain things to be healthy.

Awareness can lead to concern. As girls start to realize what the situation is, and what they can do to improve or maintain certain conditions, even the youngest of them can make decisions to act on the basis of this understanding.

Eco-Action and the accompanying patch are Girl Scouting's way to help protect the environment. Check with your Girl Scout council to find out about any Eco-Action projects or Lou Henry Hoover Memorials in your area. Or, as you and the girls explore the environment, you may discover some needs or problems that lead to your own environmental service project.

Handbook pages 298-321 lead girls to more in-depth observation of different aspects of the natural environment.

Each of these explorations can open the door to new discoveries and new adventures. They all tie in with each other as each occurs in the out-of-doors. There are activities related to: animals □ rocks and minerals □ weather □ trees □ plants (garden) □ stars and planets.

You can do these activities anywhere: city, suburbs, country. Adapt them to the environment the girls live in. Most can either be part of troop meeting activities or lead the girls on to something extra.

Use these activities as models for getting into other things the girls are interested in—wildflowers or sea shells, for instance.

Get help from local resource people and organizations when doing your explorations. Students, hobbyists, and people whose jobs are in related fields can be very helpful. Get children's families involved.

Remember, it is in doing, seeing, touching, and experiencing that girls learn the most about their world.

Note: Collecting things should be done with great care. It is wise to collect only fallen objects and not disturb growing things in their natural habitats. Some growing things are protected by law. Do you and the girls know which things these are in your area?

Try exploring in The World of Today and Tomorrow for more experiments on what things are made of and how they work.

	What to Do	Getting Ready with the Girls
Step 5	Go on a hike: it's a long walk with a purpose.	Learn the rules of the road. Decide what to take and wear. Know safety and simple first aid. Increase your distance gradually. Have a purpose in mind: trail-sign hike, sketching hike, collectors' hike, or just a hike to hike.
Step 6	Cook outdoors: it's both the fire and the food.	Try different ways of constructing a fireplace. Learn correct sizes and kinds of wood or how to use charcoal. Lay and light a fire; keep it going; then put it out. Try more than one type of cooking: one pot, skillet, stick (toasting, broiling), ember, (mud, wet paper), reflector (planking).
Step 7	Sleep outside: maybe in the "wilds" or in some one's backyard.	Plan what to take: bedding, clothing, toilet kit, flashlight, etc. Learn how to make a bedroll and pack a knapsack.
Step 8	Go camping: Emphasize campcraft here; girls learn more skills as they go.	Plan for activities at the campsite: games, explorations, what to cook, who will do what. Be safety-wise with jackknife and fires. Establish an environmentally sound campsite with: caches, latrines, cooking and sleeping quarters, homemade outdoor cooking equipment, cooking utensils, toasting forks or broilers, pothooks or cranes. Pitch and strike a tent. Handle garbage disposal and dishwashing.

Handbook pages 322-325, "Going Farther from Home," contain information that is as important for leaders as for girls.

Safety rules (handbook page 323) supplement those in *Safety-Wise.*

Play games that test girls' memories about safe ways to do things. Girls can make up their own true-or-false game or skits on safe and unsafe ways to act. One of them might want to be Suzy Safety (handbook page 5; page 30 of this leaders' guide).

Knowing where you are is an important safety feature of any hike. Discuss this before you go on a trip.

Hikes and short trips offer opportunities for girls to learn and use the eight outdoor skills of camping (handbook page 335). These skills are so important to successful outdoor living that they are repeated here:

- Know and practice good outdoor manners in town and country.
- Know how to dress for the outdoors in your locality, in relation to expected weather.
- Know how to tie, use, and release a square knot and a clove hitch.
- Know how to handle and care for a knife.
- Know how to make, use, and put out a fire for outdoor cooking.
- Know how to cook something for yourself, something for the patrol or troop.
- Know simple first aid for cuts, insect bites, skinned knees.
- Know how to protect the natural world.

Sing on the trail; it helps as you walk along and brings people together. The Girl Scout songbooks include many songs that are good for hiking.

Handbook pages 325-332 deal with finding and giving directions.

Reading a map or compass and signaling are skills that young girls enjoy learning. Practice them in a wide game or at a special outdoor event.

Wide Games

A brief explanation of wide games is given on page 332 of the handbook. There are several other things that you as leader need to know.

The main purpose of a wide game is to learn skills (or to test skills already learned) in a way that is fun.

A wide game is played by teams following a trail, with stops at several stations where specific problems are to be solved.

It is more fun if girls can be involved in the planning, but planners should not also play the game. The situation that teams discover at each stop on the trail must be a surprise to them. One patrol or a committee could work with you to make up a game for the rest of the troop.

First identify skills that the troop might be ready to try, and look over the locations available to you. (Wide games started in the out-of-doors, but they can be adapted for indoor use if you have lots of room.)

Then invent a story in which situations have to be resolved by using the skills within your chosen setting. The story does not have to be logical; indeed, fantastic ones are more exciting.

Set a time limit for activities at each station (generally no more than 10 or 15 minutes) and for the game as a whole.

See that each station has the necessary supplies, such as rope for knot tying. You will need a person to teach skills wherever that is part of the game. In any case, it may be a good idea to have someone on hand to answer questions and serve as timekeeper at each station.

You make your own rules for each game. Be sure everyone understands them. If there is to be a winning team, will they win by scoring points? by getting through the activities fastest? how else?

If there is no element of competition in the game, how will you end it? Time should be provided for girls to talk about their adventures, display anything they have made, and suggest ideas for future wide games.

Fairy tales provide good story lines for wide games. So do poems, songs, folklore, comic strips, and science fiction. Taking the example given in the handbook—a beautiful princess held captive by a wicked old witch—situations might include:

> making paper bag puppets or costumes for characters in the story
>
> using knots or lashing to create some sort of device for rescuing the princess or capturing the witch
>
> breaking a coded message sent by the princess
>
> sending back a message by Morse code telling how she will be rescued.

Additional stations might work in activities related to energy conservation, food preparation, first aid, songs, or a variety of crafts.

Camping

Many girls join Girl Scouting because they want to go camping. The joy of living out-of-doors and learning to take care of oneself, combined with the adventure of planning and living together with a group of girls, is truly exciting to them. A glimpse of girls' expectations for camping adventures is offered on page 334 of the handbook.

Page 336 of the handbook contains background information to prepare a girl for camping, both with her troop and on her own at an organized camp.

As girls grow through camping experiences, they see their own progress. This leads to a sense of self-reliance and mastery.

In the out-of-doors, a girl learns how important it is to cooperate with others and use teamwork.

Girls gain a sense of the beauty of nature and its spiritual essence as they take part in camping experiences.

On pages 337-341 of the handbook, you will find techniques and tips to use with girls in planning before a troop camping trip. Remember, as much as possible, decisions about the trip should be made by the girls.

Overnight troop camping is not always smooth and easy. There's a lot to do, but it's worth the effort.

A large part of the fun of a project is planning and anticipating it.

Encourage girls to talk about what they expect and hope for in troop camping. This is the key to activities they will plan.

Girls need to practice the skills they need for the trip, and to decide what to take along for fun and comfortable camp living.

When girls are learning new skills, either before or during a trip, they should be able to see actual results. One way to learn—and to know you have learned—is to see food cooking on the fire you have built (even if it's only hot water for soup or cocoa). A knot is only useful if it really holds or makes something.

Help girls to see the various things that need to be planned and to block out times for planning. That way they can tackle each part of a plan, and you will not have to take over at the last minute because things are not done. (See page 19 of this leaders' guide for more suggestions on planning.)

Imagining what needs to be done, and making a kaper chart (handbook page 341) to see that everything gets done, are important parts of preparing for a trip. Give girls help on identifying the jobs that need doing and assigning them in a balanced way. They can make a special list for what needs to be done in the final cleanup and pack-up.

As a special project, the girls may wish to make a permanent kaper chart board or plaque on which the names can be changed. The troop might figure out a way to waterproof their kaper chart so it is not destroyed by the elements.

Help girls think about what would be different when living out-of-doors—for example, keeping feet and head dry if it rains. Help them think of ways to be prepared, so that discomfort will not spoil their fun.

Handbook page 343 deals with protecting the natural world, an essential part of any camping activity.

Girls can become aware of the choices and adjustments that must be considered when people set up camp in the woods. Their actions at the campsite affect many other living things. Talk about what could happen in the different situations described in the handbook:

Collecting acorns takes away animals' food and seedlings.

Old logs are needed for soil decomposition and as homes for animals.

Wildflowers need to reseed, and they provide food for wild creatures.

Dishwater can upset the ecology of the pond.

Branches on bushes are homes, food, and shade for animals, and the life source of the plant.

Girls can see what happens at a site after they or others have camped there. Look closely for signs of disturbance or destruction. Help the troop leave the site looking better than they found it. Before-and-after photos could help here.

Holding a detective-hunt on the site before or after camping can help girls find clues telling them who or what was there before them.

Equipment: Girls usually bring three times as much as they need. Page 348 of the handbook contains ideas on the multiple uses of one article. Help girls see how they can share things such as toothpaste and use the same pot or other equipment for more than one purpose.

Practice making bedrolls in advance at one or more meetings. Follow the handbook illustrations on page 350 and help the girls make small ones in cloth or paper to take home. Try including the instructions, equipment list, and permission slip for parents or guardians in a packet with the miniature bedroll. Or the girls can bring all their equipment the day before the trip and help one another pack.

Handbook pages 356-372 are designed to get girls started on outdoor cooking. These are detailed instructions not only for building wood fires, but also for cooking with alternative fuels.

Consult The World of Well-Being, in the handbook and in this leaders' guide, as you help girls with meal planning. Consider variety and attractiveness, as well as nutritive value of foods. Girls could bring in color pictures of foods they like, and talk about how each is made, its value as food, the equipment needed to cook it. Consider such food alternatives as dry milk to avoid spoilage at camp.

The handbook's World of the Out-of-Doors ends with assorted camping skills and activities (pages 372-382). Here are some additional tips for you.

With older girls, you can use the flipcharts on camping skills published by GSUSA. The charts provide how-to's and safety information on several subjects: *Fire Building, Compass and Maps, Tents and Simple Shelters, Knots and Lashing,* and *Toolcraft*. They also come in handy pocket-size booklets for easy reference when camping.

Help girls learn simple skills before they learn complex ones. Trying to do tasks without needed skills results in frustration, indoors or out.

A campfire usually includes a number of activities. Build from the active to the quiet as you and the girls plan.

Look before you leap. Develop a "site profile" of the place where the group will be camping. Be familiar with such things as:

geographical and physical layout of the site (visit before camping, if possible) evacuation plan (what to do in case of fire, storm, and other emergencies)

transportation (getting in and out of camp; getting around while you are there)

the availability of water, toilets, telephone, and emergency aid

the type of shelters

the variety of possibilities for program activity.

Knowing these things, you can form a better, more practical image of what your outdoor home will be like and the kinds of adventures you might have there.

People in your Girl Scout council will acquaint you with camp regulations and required training for leaders, Girl Scout safety rules and precautions for outdoor activities (see *Safety-Wise*), and state and local regulations.

Everything that happens on a trip—traveling to and from the site, settling in, cleaning up, watching the pot, stringing the clothesline—is part of the camping experience. Girls should take as much responsibility as they are prepared for and capable of.

Keep a sense of humor, fun, and adventure. Memorable camping moments occur for girls and adults from the mistakes and work as well as from the easy times.

Page 382 of the handbook has some questions for you and the girls to think about after your trip and before you take the next one: how did it go?

Evaluation can be done informally—while waiting to be picked up at the site, in the cars going home, at the next meeting, during various parts of the event itself.

Help girls evaluate honestly. Look at the why and the how. Instead of just complaining that the food was "awful," help them think about such things as too little time spent on planning the menu, not enough practice sessions in cooking, or not enough variety in the menu. If some things went especially well, help them see how their good planning paid off. Enjoy reliving the highlights of the trip. (See page 20 of this leaders' guide, "Evaluating Learnings and Experience," for additional tips.

Outdoor Expectations

Each year, Brownie and Junior Girl Scouts should be able to look forward to a schedule that includes:

a generous number of troop meetings held out-of-doors

a series of simple cookouts

at least one all-day outing

opportunities to share outdoor skills, or to teach them to younger girls, and to participate in outdoor good turns.

Annual schedules for Junior troops should also include a troop camp experience of one or more nights.

At least once while she is a Brownie, and again as a Junior, each girl should have the opportunity to participate in a neighborhood outdoor day, and have the experience of going to day camp or a resident camp or program center.

In addition, while she is a Brownie, each girl should go troop camping for at least one night. Juniors should have the experience of planning and carrying out an outdoor play day or overnight camp involving a Brownie troop.

Brownies and Juniors will want to know that ever more challenging outdoor opportunities lie ahead. As Cadettes and Seniors they can look forward to enjoying bigger and better troop camping trips, will be taking part in council-wide or intercouncil encampments, and may even be participating in traveling camps and special events featuring high-level or high-risk skills.

Brownie and Junior Girl Scout Recognitions

There are recognitions designed for Brownie Girl Scouts and for Junior Girl Scouts. Each age level has something unique to call its very own.

For Brownie Girl Scouts there are three Brownie B patches. Each B patch shows that girls have participated as a troop in Brownie B activities during one troop year. The patches cannot be earned by individual girls.

There is also a special Bridge to Juniors patch for girls who participate in bridging activities during their last months as Brownie Girl Scouts. More information on Brownie recognitions is found starting on page 00 of this leaders' guide.

For Junior Girl Scouts there are proficiency badges, signs, and a Junior Aide patch. Individuals, small groups or patrols, or the entire troop can work towards these recognitions.

Badges are designed to encourage girls to find out about and develop skills in a wide variety of subject areas. Each badge deals with one area. It is earned when a girl can show she completed the requirements and can share her new knowledge and skill with others.

The Sign of the Arrow and the Sign of the Star lead girls into exploring many different subjects and increase their opportunities for planning, decision making, and applying the Promise and Law. A sign is a more involved project than a badge and might take an entire troop a year to complete.

The Junior Aide patch is a symbol of assistance to Brownie Girl Scouts who are ready to bridge to Juniors.

Recognitions for Brownie and Junior Girl Scouts are meant to enrich the Girl Scout program. They are not essentials. You can have an exciting, well-balanced troop program with or without them. Just keep in mind that working toward recognitions should fit into the total picture of troop activity.

Girls will look to you, as their partner in planning, for help in deciding whether and when to work on badges, signs, or patch activities. They will also appreciate your suggestions of specific badge subjects or Brownie B patch activities.

To be an effective adviser on these matters, you need to be thoroughly familiar with the requirements for recognitions available to your troop's age level. If you are also sensitive to special interests and talents—of the group and of individuals—it is not hard to help the girls sort out activities and requirements that will be the most rewarding.

Make Adaptations When Needed

Recognitions give girls a variety of activities from which to choose. In addition to built-in choices, requirements for most recognitions allow for adaptation according to individual and group situations, including: geography or climate ▢ available local resources ▢ special opportunities or limitations of the group and its members.

It is neither realistic nor desirable to expect that every girl who wears a Girl Scout patch, badge, or sign will have done exactly the same things in exactly the same way as every other girl who wears that symbol.

The point of making adaptations is to personalize requirements, not to simplify them. Ask yourself and the girls if changes are being suggested merely because a requirement is difficult. If that is the case, help them see how they could do the requirement without adapting it. Ask:

What do you need to know in order to do this requirement?

How could you find this out or learn it?

Who or what could help you?

When the girls and you have answered these questions, help them plan ways to find out about the subject or learn the necessary skills. It might mean setting aside time at troop meetings, or having a girl or group of girls work on their own, with you, or with a special consultant.

Most requirements call for investigation, preparation, and/or practice. If you help the girls to understand this and fulfill the requirements honestly, everyone will feel more satisfied.

When you and the girls are in doubt as to how much adaptation can be made, or whether a recognition has been earned, go back to the stated purpose of the recognition.

For tips about your role in the choosing process, see "Making Choices," pages 18-19 of this leaders' guide.

Specific help on Brownie patches follows directly. Specific help on Junior badges, signs, and the Junior Aide patch starts on page 73.

Especially for Brownie Girl Scouts

The official Brownie patches are a form of non-competitive recognition to be worked on by the entire Brownie Girl Scout troop. They are designed to:

° recognize participation, not performance

° encourage girls and leaders to select, plan, and carry out a well-rounded variety of troop activities based on the three Brownie B's, as described in the handbook:

Be a Discoverer

Be a Ready Helper

Be a Friend-Maker

Within the framework of the three B's, girls can plan and carry out activities from the five Worlds of interest and activities especially related to being a Girl Scout. Sample activities in each of these categories are given on pages 63-67 of the handbook. A much larger selection appears on pages 65-72 of this leaders' guide.

Each Brownie B patch represents a year of participation in Brownie B activities. A girl receives a separate patch for each year she participates:

First year: yellow patch

Second year: red patch

Third year: blue patch

As a troop, girls will be doing the same or similiar activities; but they may receive different colored patches depending on how many years they have participated in the Brownie B plan. For example, a girl who joins Brownies as a second grader would receive a yellow patch at the end of her first year. Other second graders, who have participated the year before, would be getting the red or second patch for the same activities. The color of the patch does not relate directly to the age or grade of the Brownie.

To get a Brownie B patch, the troop completes a total of 12 activities. For variety and balance, your 12 selections should include:

° at least one activity from each of the Brownie B's.

° at least one activity about Girl Scouting and one from each World.

Using a checklist like the one that follows will help you keep track of the pattern each year. As the troop completes an activity for the patch, put a check in the appropriate box. Make the chart a big one, so everyone can see the progress.

Other ways to help the girls see their progress in working toward each B patch are:

a troop Brownie B activity scrapbook

a pictorial progress poster

Patch Pattern

Have at least one check after each of these	Have at least one check in each of these three columns			Total number of activities
	Discoverer	Ready Helper	Friend-Maker	
About Girl Scouting	1 3	1 3	1 3	
World of Well-Being	1 3			1
World of People	1 3			1
World of Today and Tomorrow				
World of the Arts	1 3			2
World of the Out-of-Doors	1 3			1
Total (12 or more)				7

a display or skit to show and tell visitors about the B activities the troop has done

individual memory books in which girls record the B activities they've done. Pictures and/or words about each activity might follow a simple format such as this:

World of _____

☐ **Discoverer**   ☐ **Ready Helper**   ☐ **Friend-Maker**

What we did _____

_____

What I did _____

_____

What was fun _____

_____

As activities are selected, keep in mind a balance of types: active and quiet, indoor and outdoor, at the meeting place and away.

Brownie B patches can help girls build on previous experiences as they try new things. There may be similar activities listed in each of the three Brownie B's, but one activity should not be checked off more than once within a single year. For example, if the girls did something to improve their meeting place as Ready Helpers one year, they can choose to do that activity again another year—doing it in a different or more complex way, or continuing from what they did the previous year.

You and your troop select and plan your patch activities based on everyone's interests and abilities. Here are some examples.

Troop A wishes to sample all of the Worlds and all of the Brownie B's as widely as possible. They do two activities about Girl Scouting and two in each of the five Worlds, with an even mixture of four Discoverer, four Friend-Maker, and four Ready Helper activities.

The girls in Troop B like the idea of being Discoverers. They do two activities about Girl Scouting and two in each of the Worlds, but among the twelve activities they do only one Ready Helper, three Friend-Makers, and eight Discoverers.

Troop C is especially interested in people and the out-of-doors. They do four activities in each of these Worlds, one in each of the three remaining Worlds, and one about Girl Scouting. They do a mixture of four Discoverer, five Friend-Maker, and three Ready Helper activities.

In Troop D, the girls in their last year as Brownies are particularly eager to be Discoverers and Friend-Makers in Junior Girl Scouting. They also want to be Ready Helpers with the new Brownies in their troop. They do seven activities about Girl Scouting, one as Discoverers, three as Friend-Makers, and three as Ready Helpers. They also

do five other Discoverer activities, one in each of the five Worlds of interest.

How to Get Started

Start with the girls' ideas. Keep a chart or list of things the Brownies say they would like to do. Once you can identify a World that especially appeals to them, you will be able to find Brownie B activities in this leaders' guide (or in the handbook) that relate to the girls' expressed interests.

Another way is to use the Brownie B activities as idea-starters. Ask the girls to select one of the three B's and one World that they particularly like. Then present suggested activities from the handbook and from this leaders' guide in one of the following ways:

describe them orally, for discussion by the troop;

print them on index cards for the girls to sort through;

print them on a blackboard or a large sheet of paper;

let older Brownies read activities from this leaders' guide;

for younger Brownies, show a drawing, photograph, or clipping to start discussion.

As with any activity, use your own awareness of the girls' abilities and readiness in helping them to decide among these suggestions. Girls may want (or be able) to do only some parts of an activity.

Some of the Brownie B activities, such as making visits or inviting guests, will call for special arrangements ahead of time.

Brownie B Activities

The following activities, and those given on pages 63-67 of the handbook, represent various degrees of complexity so that girls can work at the level of their own abilities. Those marked with an asterisk (*) are most appropriate for beginning Brownies.
Girls, not you as leader, are the "you" in these suggested troop activities.

About Girl Scouting

Be a Discoverer
* Learn several Girl Scout songs, including the "Brownie Smile Song," "Whene'er You Make a Promise," the "Brownie Hiking Song," and a grace.

Learn and practice how to take care of flags. Learn a little about the history of the flag. Take part in a flag ceremony. Each girl should have a chance to carry and attend the flag. Learn and sing a patriotic song.

Choose a country where there are Girl Guides (see resource list, page 79 of leaders' guide). Visit a travel agent or someone who has been to that country. Ask her or him to tell you about traveling there, what sights you might see, food you might eat, how you could get there, and how long it would take. Find out how much it might cost.

Make a list of Brownie Girl Scout manners. Discuss them in your Brownie Ring and practice them on a trip and at troop meetings. Act out good and bad manners.

Play a "getting acquainted" game to learn the names (or something else about them) of each of the girls in the troop. Learn and sing "Make New Friends." Or trace a friend's body on large paper. Then draw or paint her in a Brownie uniform.

Visit the Girl Scout council office in your area or invite a Girl Scout staff member to come and tell you what adults do to help Girl Scouts. Find out why leaders volunteer to do their job and what they do to get ready for meetings. Think up a way to thank them.

Find your council's camp or camps on a map. Plan and go on a day trip to one of the camps. Go on a discovery hike while you're there.

Be a Ready Helper

Do something to help take care of or improve your meeting place. Discuss what doing a good turn means. Sample projects might be:

Make posters, reminding everyone to help keep the meeting place neat and clean.

Design and make a decoration for the room, such as a mural.

Provide and decorate waste baskets.

Help care for the grounds.

If you need suggestions, invite the person responsible for the meeting place to visit one of your meetings.

Help out at special services on Girl Scout Sunday or Sabbath at your place of worship. Wear your uniform, so everyone can see that you are a Girl Scout.

Be a helper in your troop. Write up a list of troop jobs. Make a plan for rotating the jobs. Try using a kaper chart.

Make posters about Girl Scouting to help encourage other girls to join. Put them up in places where girls will see them: stores, schools, churches, libraries.

Collect used stamps for the Stamp Bank in Norway. It assists Girl Guide Associations in need throughout the world. Pack stamps in good condition in a box marked "Used Postage Stamps," so it can enter Norway duty free. Mail to the Stamp Bank, Box 104, 1601 Fredrikstad, Norway.

Make a special display (for a public place) that shows what Brownies do for Girl Scout Week.

Find out the many wonderful ways the Juliette Low World Friendship Fund helps Girl Scouts and Girl Guides in this and other countries. Try to find a Senior, Campus Girl Scout, or older person who has been on an international project assisted by the JLWFF. Ask her to tell about the fund and her experience. Find ways for each girl to contribute to the JLWFF at a special ceremony.

Be a Friend-Maker

Learn about the Girl Scout special days and participate in a neighborhood or council event on one of those days.

Invite a Junior, Cadette, or Senior Girl Scout to a Brownie meeting. Ask her to show you her uniform and handbook and to tell you what she does in Girl Scouting (and did when she was a Brownie).

Invite senior citizens to come to a Brownie meeting. Tell them what Brownies do; sing some Brownie songs for them. Ask the senior citizens to teach or tell you about something they enjoy.

Keep a scrapbook of some of your Brownie fun. Show the scrapbook to new girls and visitors to troop meetings.

Be a friend-maker with another Brownie troop by visiting or exchanging a newspaper or troop letter. Each girl can write or draw something to share.

In the spring, invite girls who will be new Brownies in the fall to your meeting. Tell them what to expect as a Brownie. (Find out if their mothers or fathers would also like to come.) Or visit a kindergarten class and tell the girls about Brownies. Show them samples of what you've made, pictures of what you've done, and places you've visited. Teach the class a simple song or game.

Be pen friends with Brownies in other troops in your council or in another council. Share your experiences with them. Try something in your troop that the other troop thought was great fun.

Make up a quiz game about the parts of the Girl Scout Law. Play it with another troop. (Save it to help new girls learn the Law, too.)

Plan and hold a cookout, special party, or game day with another troop.

Choose a few countries of the World Association of Girl Guides and Girl Scouts and locate them on a map. Find out what name their Brownies use and what their pin looks like. Try learning to say the Promise in their language. Find out how these Brownies might have fun; learn some of the songs, dances, crafts, holidays, or customs of these international friends. Make a scrapbook of what you learn. Include a map or flag. Add magazine pictures of girls, drawings of houses, clothing, animals, flowers, birds, trees, and holiday customs.

Visit a Junior troop meeting and do one or more of the following:

Share a song, game, or dance with them.

Learn about badges and signs.

Learn campcraft skills from the Juniors.

Spend a day outdoors with a Junior troop.

Have a bridging ceremony followed by a party for both troops.

In addition, the following activities from the handbook may be counted as Brownie patch requirements for About Girl Scouting:

Pages 10-11	Understanding the Girl Scout Law
Page 14	Good turns (service projects)
Page 28	Follow in Daisy's footsteps
Pages 29-31	Observance of special days
Page 37	Scouts' Own
Page 39	Flag ceremony

World of Well-Being

Be a Discoverer
* Have a troop tasting party. Try several foods you've never had before.

Find out what vaccinations you have had. Ask a doctor, nurse, or other health care professional to talk to the troop about why vaccinations are necessary. Make and keep a personal health chart for yourself; include daily personal care routine, sleep, exercise, meals, and snacks.

Find out what adults you know enjoy doing in their spare time. See how many of these things they also did when they were children. Have a few parents teach you about their hobbies.

Learn and practice how to light and put out a campfire safely. Learn at least three different types of fires Girl Scouts use when they go camping. What are the special safety rules for each?

* Chart your growth measurements over a few months and compare them with those of a baby.

Visit a veterinarian, local animal shelter, zoo, or farm. Find out what shots the animals get and why. If possible, find out what foods they eat and how they take care of their young.

Plan a snack for a special occasion. Figure out how much of each ingredient will be needed and how much it will cost. Then shop for the items. See if the cost is what you expected.

Make a safety check of the troop's meeting place. Also check at home. Discuss the things Brownies can do to change things that are unsafe and then do them.

Find out what foods are good for you. Plan and prepare by yourself a lunch to take on a Brownie outing.

Take care of some parts of your home on a regular basis.

Make a troop dream diary using pictures or words. Dream about what you want to be or want to do in Girl Scouting. Try to meet someone doing what you dream about, an adult or an older Girl Scout, and ask her or him to tell you what it's like.

Be a Ready Helper
* Discuss and make posters to show good safety rules for traveling by foot, bike, car, or public transportation. Display them where other young people will see them (schools, pediatrician's office, dentist's office, library, stores, etc.).

* Do something extra special for someone who is ill.

Learn and play several new games. Include at least one international game and find out as much as you can about the children who play it. Teach the games to another group; tell them where the international game came from, and about the children who play it.

Help clean up a playground or small park in your area.

Make up and put on skits about health and safety for small children.

Hold a story hour once or twice for small children in your neighborhood.

Show younger or new girls in the troop what is in the troop first aid kit and how to use the items. Make personal first aid kits to be used at home and on troop and family outings.

Be a Friend-Maker
* Make something attractive and useful to decorate your troop meeting place, some place in your community, or your home.

* Entertain some younger children by singing, acting, or playing with them.

* Find out the dates of family events, such as birthdays and anniversaries, and make a personal calendar. Plan to do something to make one family member feel special on one of these occasions. Share what you've done with others in the troop.

Find out what makes a toy safe and fun for an infant or toddler. Make some toys and play with the children.

Have a family game day for the troop members' families. Play games that all ages can enjoy together.

* Do some Brownie good turns at home that help to make your home safer or family members happier.

Do something to beautify your neighborhood or meeting place. Plant some flowers, clean up an area, paint, or make something useful.

Invite handicapped girls to participate in a troop activity.

Attend a sports event where girls or women are the participants. Talk to an athlete (or team). Try to find out how she prepares for the game. Have her show you some basic skills of the game and try them yourself.

Visit a recreational area where there is swimming. Talk to the lifeguard about safety in the water. Find out about the "buddy system."

Have each girl show, tell, or teach the rest of the troop something she really enjoys doing.

In addition, the following activities from the handbook may be counted as Brownie patch requirements in The World of Well-Being:

Page 86	What's special about you and others
Page 88	Family collage
Page 88	Guessing game, things girls can be
Page 89	Special "thank you" note
Page 89	Draw how you feel
Page 90	"Me" puppet
Page 95	Hazard hunt
Page 96	Wheel of fitness
Page 97	"Time to stretch" games
Page 99	Walk like an animal
Page 102	Bicycle care and safe driving
Page 108	Helping at home
Page 112	Household mysteries
Page 116	Tasting party
Page 118	Snack hunt and "Poor Snack" games
Page 120	Making a sit-upon
Page 124	Emergency who's who

The World of People

Note: In planning family-oriented activities, take care to be sensitive to girls' individual situations.

Be a Discoverer

* Have a Family Day to share family activities, foods, or customs.

* Discuss different ways decisions are made in families. How do these ways differ from the way decisions are made in a Brownie Ring? Use Brownie Ring for planning and deciding on activities for meetings.

Visit important community spots, historical buildings and locations, and recreational sites. Learn about each location. Make pictures, songs, stories, or poems to tell about what you have seen.

Visit some of the oldest and newest houses and buildings in your community. Make models of some of these buildings. Or make a model of the house, farm, or apartment where you live (or the garage, one room, or the yard) to share with your troop. (Your model might be used as a dollhouse afterwards.)

Visit people in your community who come from another country or who represent a minority group, and who have a special skill. Learn about their skill and their people. Or invite such a person to your troop meeting to share this information.

* Talk about and write or draw the answers to these questions: "If I could be any person I wanted to be, who would I be? Where would I live? What would I be doing?" Or, "If I could change five things to make the world a better place to live, I would change..."

Find out how decisions about parks, schools, and streets are made in your community. Talk with community officials and members of the League of Women Voters about this. Ask to see a voting machine and learn how it works.

Work together to make up an imaginary country. (It may be helpful to study a real country first.) Make a map of the imaginary country, flat or three-dimensional. Design a flag. Figure out what weather the country has, what the flowers, trees, or animals are like, and what the people eat. Make models of their houses and other buildings. Make up clothing, games, or songs. Give a play or puppet show to tell about your imaginary country.

Visit museums, historical societies, folk art galleries, union halls, places of worship, ethnic festivals, or cultural community centers to learn more about the cultures represented in your area and each one's special contribution to our country.

Invite an exchange student from another country at a local high school or a nearby university to come to your meeting to tell about his or her country or culture. (Guidance counselors or a Foreign Student Office can put you in touch with these young people.)

Visit a grocery store with an international counter, or a bakery, restaurant, or delicatessen that specializes in foods from another country, to find out what is available in your community. Learn which foods that you eat regularly come from other countries. Try some foods you've never eaten before. Choose a few countries (ones where there are Girl Guides) and make a list of the foods from these countries that you can buy locally.

Find out how UNICEF and other organizations help children around the world.

Be a Ready Helper

* Make a list of all the ways girls think they can be of help in the neighborhood and to family members. Post a list, drawn up by the girls, of helping activities they have done for their families and friends.

Take part in a community program that is appropriate for Brownies.

Assist younger Brownies in your own or another troop to learn more about being a Brownie. Teach them a game, song, or dance, or take them someplace special to share something already learned.

Set up a simple project of collecting stamps, books, or magazines, which you can send to organizations assisting people in other parts of the world. (See page 79 of this leaders' guide for resources.)

* List ways to be "good neighbors," and carry out a troop project using some of these ways.

Make toys children played with 100 to 200 years ago. If possible, visit a historical society, doll museum, or children's museum for ideas or assistance. Or mend toys you played with and give them to a children's center.

Help a Senior Girl Scout get ready for a visit to Girl Guides or Girl Scouts in another country. (Telephone your council to find out about Seniors in your area.) Make some simple gifts and swaps she can take to children in her host family. Ask her to tell you about her travels before and after the trip.

Be a Friend-Maker

* Give parties for each other and for your families.

* Find ways to be friends to a family member who may need special help.

Play hostesses to a new family or their children. Share with them what you know about your community.

Get in touch with handicapped or elderly people who would be made happy by Brownie visits or could share in Brownie outings or activities.

Have a "Brownie Afternoon" to hostess a Girl Guide or Girl Scout or other international visitor to your council. Exchange information about Brownies, school activities, games, or crafts of your countries.

* Bring a friend or family members to a troop outing or a special meeting.

Help collect or make clothing, food, or toys for a community project.

* Learn a few words in the language of someone the girls in the troop meet with frequently. Or learn a few words in the language of a visitor to the troop from another country or cultural group.

In addition, the following activities from the handbook may be counted as Brownie patch requirements in The World of People:

The World of Today and Tomorrow

Be a Discoverer

* Visit a factory, farm, garage, or office, wherever there are machines, to learn how the machines and the people who operate them work.

* Visit a railroad station or an airport. Go up into the signal or control tower. See the inside of a railway locomotive or the cockpit of an airplane. Learn about some of the signaling devices, how the pilot operates a train or plane, how it moves forward and backwards, a few important parts of the locomotive or plane.

* Invent a toy or game of odds and ends and use it. Or make a kite or pinwheel that works, using objects found out-of-doors. Or make something from another country or another time in the past or future.

Visit a telephone company to see the operators at work and find out about the switchboard. Learn how they place calls, including one overseas. Or visit an electrical power plant to see the generators at work. Learn where the power comes from and where it goes, and how to make better use of it.

Learn to use some audiovisual (AV) equipment: a tape recorder, record player, filmstrip projector, film loop projector. Perhaps your council office will let you visit and learn to use their AV equipment.

Ask a parent or automobile mechanic to show the girls what is underneath a car's hood. Identify these parts: radiator and radiator cap, battery, engine block, fan and fan belt, oil dip stick, windshield washer fluid, and spark plugs. Be able to recognize and name these parts in two or three different cars. Try to have someone show you a car with a small engine and one with a large engine.

Build a model plane and fly it, or put together a model train or car so it will run. Or build a model airport, put together a train track or highway system, and make a safety sign for it.

Visit a restaurant, bakery, or school cafeteria to compare the equipment they use to that used in your home for cooking and baking. (If girls have learned to measure with ease, they can compare the height or width of pans and bowls from home with those used commercially.)

Learn, if possible, to use a simple calculator. Use it to count troop dues. Use the calculator to determine the cost of refreshments or amount of ingredients needed for a party or an outing.

Go on a scavenger or treasure hunt with metric clues such as: Walk ahead 3 meters and turn right at the rock 15 cm high. Find a pebble 2 cm wide.

Take the bulbs and batteries out of several flashlights. Mix them with several different-sized batteries and bulbs, some that work and some that don't. Have everyone reassemble the flashlights so that they all light.

Talk with a school, church, or apartment building custodian. Find out about his or her work to keep the place in running order, about his or her tools, and how to use them.

Be a Ready Helper

* Learn to clean and to properly grease, oil, or silicone spray the necessary points on your bicycle. Help a friend or younger child to clean up and fix his or her bicycle.

* Learn to use simple home repair tools: pliers, screwdriver, wrench, hammer, and saw. Help make simple repairs at home.

Learn how to use a household appliance, such as a washing machine or vacuum cleaner, and help a family member do this job several times.

Make some inventions: to clean up the meeting place faster, to make getting up in the morning more fun, to carry things on your head, to teach a small child to count or learn her ABC's, etc.

Make a time capsule for a future Brownie troop filled with Discoverer ideas and ways to be Ready Helpers and Friend-Makers. Arrange with your council to store the time capsule and have it opened in two or three years.

Be a Friend-Maker

* Visit the council office on a day when most of the staff are there to tell how their jobs help girls. Find out what machines they have and how the machines are operated.

Make model airplanes, cars, buses, trains, or other toys from wood or cardboard cartons and give them to children's hospitals or homes.

Construct a simple stage set. Put on a skit for another troop, parents, senior citizens, or younger children.

Tape-record stories or songs for people who would especially enjoy them, such as senior citizens, younger children, handicapped or hospitalized persons.

Make something useful of wood and give it to a friend or family member.

In addition, the following activities from the handbook may be counted as Brownie patch requirements in The World of Today and Tomorrow:

The World of the Arts

Be a Discoverer

* Make a simple stencil. Try different ways of using stencils, such as brushing on paint, spattering paint or ink using a toothbrush, dabbing on paint with a sponge.

* Using simple shapes, explore making a border design and an overall design. Draw or cut out shapes or make a stamp print with different objects, such as spool, carrot, eraser.

Create a three-dimensional circus, zoo, or aquarium by making figures out of cardboard or heavy paper and mounting them inside a box or on a box lid.

* Look for stories about elves, pixies, fairies, trolls, leprechauns, brownies, etc., in legends and folk tales from around the world. Make a collection of pictures of what you imagine they would look like and make up stories about them. Later, act out the stories just for fun.

Attend a dance or music recital, musical play, children's theater, band concert, operetta, festival of ethnic music and dance. Discuss some of the parts you enjoyed and would like to do someday. Draw a picture of what you saw, make up a play or puppet show about it, or learn the songs.

At an art museum or gallery, or in art books, look at still life pictures. Afterwards, make an arrangement of fruit, vegetables, leaves, or flowers, and draw or paint it.

Visit a church or other building to see stained glass or mosaic. If possible, have someone explain or show how these art forms are made. Make stained glass designs using colored tissue paper and black construction paper. Or make a mosaic design by gluing cut-up pieces of colored construction paper onto cardboard.

Plan and act out a TV commercial for a product you wish to sell.

Learn to do a square or folk dance. Participate in a dance get-together with Juniors or another troop.

Collect as many different styles of lettering as you can from magazines, boxes, newspapers. Make some practice sheets of lettering. Try lettering something with the style you like best on a card, poster, sign, booklet, nameplate, etc.

Make and use a tape recording of different musical sounds as background for a play or puppet show the troop gives. Your singing, your performance on an instrument, or parts of records you own could be taped.

Be a Ready Helper

* Make friendship bags for hospitalized children. Include:

    a cardboard loom with enough yarn to make something

    a bag labeled "Watch Out! Fierce Animal Inside!" and containing a piece of plasticene for the child to use in creating an animal

    a puppet to keep the child company and for putting on plays with roommates

    a drawing board with sheets of paper to fit it and crayons or markers

    a bag of beads and a cord to string them.

* Design and make rhythm instruments for younger children. Teach the younger children how to use the instruments and teach them songs or singing games to go along with the instruments.

Gather natural materials and make a decorative arrangement. Or make a simple flower arrangement using different colors and kinds of weeds, grasses, or flowers and present it for a public place, special occasion, or Girl Scout ceremony.

Read folk tales from other countries. Retell them to little children. You might include illustrations, scenery, costumes, or actions to liven up the stories.

Make hand puppets of different family members. Get in touch with your local family services agency to find out if they can use the puppets.

Make picture flash cards, texture games, or "dressing cards" (snaps, buttons, shoelaces) for younger children.

Be a Friend-Maker

* Create a greeting card, wrapping paper, writing paper, or place mats for a new friend; use any art form you like.

* Make decorations for a holiday or community event (painted eggs for a "welcome spring" tree; dolls in handmade period costumes for the fourth of July; paper flowers; valentines; Brownie art exhibit; photographs), and place them where people will enjoy seeing them.

As a joint troop project, work on a dollhouse or room. Decide colors for walls, floor, curtains; make furniture, etc. Make tiny dolls to put in the room. Share your house with others who would enjoy it.

Make up a short play. Design your own scenery and costumes if possible. Act it out and take color slides or draw pictures of the scenes. Add a script to your slides or pictures and show them to an audience.

Visit an art museum. Talk to someone who works there. Find out how pieces of art are taken care of. Find out what things people can do at an art museum.

In addition, the following activities from the handbook may be counted as Brownie patch requirements in The World of the Arts:

The World of the Out-of-Doors

Be a Discoverer

* Each Brownie bring a one-meter piece of clothesline (about three feet) to troop meeting. Learn simple knots and what they are used for at camp. Play some knot games and relays.

* Discover what is underneath where you walk: animal burrows, mole holes, underground water, sewer pipes, or subways. Make drawings of what you think that unseen, underground world looks like.

* Talk about Suzy Safety in the Brownie Ring. Make a list of ways Brownie Girl Scouts can take care of themselves on hikes, during the troop meetings, and at camp. Make a troop first aid kit and plan how to and how not to use it.

Visit a sewage disposal plant, a dump or land fill, a power company, an oil refinery, a recycling center. Find out what your community is doing to deal with pollution and waste.

Practice the metric system while camping and using outdoor skills; try measuring length of pace, hiking distance, liquid quantities for cooking. Use metric measures for the length of knotting ropes and mark them on cups and hiking sticks.

Using compass direction, draw a map of the troop's favorite outdoor spot, marking its special features so others can find, enjoy, and protect them.

Make a macrame hanging or necklace using, if possible, objects discovered during appreciation hikes or during a visit to a favorite spot.

Spend a day at a Girl Scout camp testing the outdoor skills learned and practicing new ones. Make plans in troop meetings on where to go, what to do, equipment needed, cost, who will help, how to get there, what to wear, and other details important for the adventure.

Be a Ready Helper

* Take care of a small pond, stream, neighborhood park, church, or schoolyard throughout a season.

* Make a plant cutting or start a new plant from a potato or carrot to give to someone.

* Ask a naturalist to visit the troop to talk about the plants, trees, and flowers that wildlife need for food and shelter. Plan ways to attract the creatures you want to live near you by planting their favorite vegetation. Find out how planting certain plants or introducing certain predators can discourage pests and what you can do to work toward a natural balance of the environment at your favorite spot.

If you can, start a troop project to raise a farm animal, small or large, to send to a community in another country.

Find out what wildlife in your community is protected by law. Make posters or booklets to tell people about them and to enlist help in protecting them. Visit a zoo, a museum of natural history, a wildlife sanctuary, a college or university, and talk to people about endangered species in other parts of the world.

Start a backyard or doorstep vegetable garden, or help organize a neighborhood garden spot. Share the vegetables you grow with senior citizens or others in your community.

Be a Friend-Maker

* Share the wonder of the out-of-doors each season with people who cannot be outside. Make and give them an original craft item, poem, story, or song that reflects the season out-of-doors.

As a troop, think up some outdoor games or devices you can use to help others learn the metric system. Use them during a program or hike with other people.

* Bring friends interested in becoming Brownies to visit the troop. Plan activities that include introducing the girls to the troop's favorite outdoor spot.

Make a booklet of near and not-so-near places of interest the troop has visited or has learned about. Tell how to get there, whom to get in touch with, what to expect, and what the troop enjoyed most. Trade your booklet for one from a troop in another neighborhood or district of the council, and test out some of the discoveries they have made. Or start and add to a list of places Brownie Girl Scouts would enjoy visiting in your neighborhood.

Make a collage, sun print, spatter print, or drawing of several things that live in the same habitat. These prints or designs may be gifts for friends or for someone who has helped the troop. Or make plaster casts of several different animal tracks to give someone.

In addition, the following activities from the handbook may be counted as Brownie patch requirements in The World of the Out-of-Doors:

Page 289	Favorite outdoor spot
Pages 289-290	Bees and butterflies
	That's my leaf
	Listening post
	Stake a claim
	Animal home hike
Page 296	Eco-action
Page 299	Animals where you live
Page 305	Bird watching
Page 308	Salt crystals experiment
Page 308	Prospectors' hike
Page 314	Neighborhood trees
Page 315	Planting experiments
Page 322	Walk around the block
Page 335	Outdoor skills
Page 348	Bandana tricks
Page 350	Bedroll
Page 360	Buddy burner
Page 368	Campfire stew
Page 365	Fire starters
Pages 377-380	Using the jackknife

The Bridge to Juniors Patch

Brownies often need help and encouragement in "crossing the bridge" into Junior Girl Scouting. As a girl nears the end of Brownies, she might have some fears and doubts about meeting new girls and adult leaders. She may wonder about the program activities. She may not be certain of her welcome in a new troop.

The Bridge to Juniors patch encourages a Brownie to meet and get to know Junior Girl Scouts and find out about the program at their age level. The ultimate aim of the Bridge to Juniors activities is for the girl to feel accepted by new friends in a new troop and to feel that her interests will be recognized and shared by others.

These activities are also an opportunity for Juniors to show their skills in planning and reaching out to others. Junior Girl Scouts can earn a Junior Aide patch by participating in and organizing Brownie bridging activities. (See pages 74-75 in this section of the leaders' guide for more information on the Junior Aide patch.)

How the Patch is Earned

The Bridge to Juniors patch is earned through participation in the special bridging activities described on pages 67-68 in the handbook and page 72 of this leaders' guide. To receive a Bridge to Juniors patch, the older Brownies in a troop carry out at least four of these bridging activities. As with the Brownie B activities, these suggestions may be modified or added to as appropriate.

Participants are Brownies who will be moving into Junior Girl Scouting at the end of the year. Bridge to Juniors activities usually occur during the last months of Brownie Girl Scout meetings.

Girls and adults plan Bridge to Juniors activities together. In troops that have Brownies of different ages, the co-leader or another adult may work with the older girls separately in planning and carrying out the activities. The girls who will soon become Juniors can form a "bridging group" for this purpose.

Personal contact with Junior Girl Scouts is a major part of bridging activities. If you don't already have bridging arrangements, get in touch with your Girl Scout council to find out about the who's and where's of Junior troops in your area. Make sure that people in both troops, Brownie and Junior, know about bridging plans and about what everybody will be doing. Share the goals of the bridging Brownies with the Junior troop leader so that she can help the Juniors understand and carry out their roles. Get-acquainted games, name tags, and a special "sister" from the other troop are especially helpful.

Bridge to Juniors Activities

Plan and carry out a joint activity with a Junior troop you have invited.

Invite someone from a Junior troop to come to your troop and tell you about Juniors, teach a song, game, etc.

Look in the Junior Badges and Signs book at the first requirement for these badges: Dabbler, Health Aid, Hospitality, Magic Carpet, My Community, My Home, My Trefoil. Discuss with your bridging group which one of these requirements you would like to try. Start working on the activity in the spring, during the summer, or at camp. Work on it alone, with other Brownies who are flying up, or with a Junior buddy.

Visit a Junior troop meeting. Find out something you didn't know about Juniors. Talk in your bridging group afterwards about the things you learned.

Help plan and participate in a service project being done by a Junior troop.

Hold an activity for new or prospective Brownies and be big sisters. Make the younger girls feel welcome and teach them a favorite song or game. Tell them about the Brownie B's, the Brownie Ring, and the Brownie Story.

Know the eight outdoor skills (page 335 of the handbook, page 60 of this leaders' guide). Use each skill to do or make something.

Especially for Junior Girl Scouts

Badges

Brownie Girl Scouts look ahead with eager anticipation to earning badges as Junior Girl Scouts. Badges can be an exciting extension of the Girl Scout program, providing opportunities for individuals, small groups or patrols, and the whole troop to be creative. You can help girls to make the most of these opportunities by placing the emphasis on carrying out the stated purpose of each badge and being able to share what is learned with others. Earning badges should not become a game of "who earned the most, fastest."

New Junior Girl Scouts might need very little encouragement to work on badges, but they will need help getting started and selecting what they are interested in exploring. You will feel more secure about offering this advice if you have studied the book *Worlds to Explore: Junior Badges and Signs*. Girls will expect you to be familiar with "Some Steps You Can Take to Choose and Earn Badges" on pages 12-13 of the book. In addition, if you read the requirements for all of the badges, you will probably find that you are automatically matching some badges with interests you know girls have.

Here are some ways to get started:

Have a badge-sampling wide game (see page 60 of this leaders' guide). Girls could try simple requirements selected from a variety of badges in different subject areas. This can help them find badges they would like to earn.

Point out to girls that they are already doing some badge requirements as a part of week-to-week activities they have planned. Once they have done a requirement or two, they will probably enjoy finishing the badge.

If individuals or a small group are enthusiastic about something the rest of the troop is not interested in, encourage them to work on a badge that relates to the special interest.

When you know the badge requirements, you can point out ways that one badge leads to another in an ever-widening circle of interests. You will also see how badges can be part of blazing a program trail with your troop (see chart on page 21 of this leaders' guide).

Always encourage girls to use badges as starting points, not as ends in themselves. After requirements are completed, help girls to expand their knowledge even more by taking related trips, planning service projects using the skills and knowledge gained, or learning more advanced skills in the same field.

Our Own Troop's _____ Badge

When the girls in the troop have an interest for which no badge is given in *Junior Badges and Signs*, they can develop a special badge. The subject of the badge should be approved by the council, but requirements must be developed by the girls under your guidance.

The great value in this badge is creation of the requirements by girls themselves for their own special use. It is also important that the girls design and execute the badge symbol, which may not be worn by anyone except themselves.

It is essential that girls have successful experience earning a variety of other proficiency badges before developing an Our Own Troop's _____ Badge.

You Don't Have To Know It All

Although you do need to know what activities are included in each badge, no leader is expected to be able to help girls with the content of every badge. This is where your co-leader and consultants can be especially helpful. By relying on the talents and special interests of other adults as badge consultants, you introduce girls to new adult friends as well as to potential hobbies and careers.

Signs

It is an easy step from earning badges in specific areas to earning signs, which encourage activity in a wide variety of areas and lead Junior Girl Scouts into increased planning and decision making. A sign could take from a few months to an entire troop year, and includes opportunities for group as well as individual activities.

There are two ways to earn both the Sign of the Arrow and the Sign of the Star: the Traditional Way and the New Way. Both ways provide girls with activities to choose from. The New Way encourages greater independence on the part of the girls and offers more choices.

The Sign of the Arrow is often earned before the Sign of the Star, but is not a prerequisite for it.

Girls in their second year of Junior Girl Scouting are usually ready to start working on one of the signs.

Goal Setting for and Evaluation of Badges and Signs

Girls will need your help to set realistic standards of performance and accomplishment for themselves as they earn badges and signs. To avoid frustration and disappointment—for yourself as well as for the girls—make sure you have an agreement ahead of time on what it is reasonable to accomplish in each badge (or sign) a girl decides to work on. Such an agreement should be made before work on a recognition is too far under way. It should be a blend of expectations: yours for the girl and the girl's for herself. Help girls set their standards high, but not so high that success may be impossible.

When you and a girl are deciding whether a badge or sign has been earned, progress should be measured against the girl's own past performance. Growth is a personal, not a competitive, matter.

Space for recording the completion of each requirement and for the signature of girl and leader are provided in the *Junior Badges and Signs* book. This record helps a girl see her total accomplishments and is helpful if she moves to another troop or if leadership changes.

Junior Aide Patch

The Junior Aide patch represents active assistance, as a Junior Girl Scout, to Brownies who are bridging.

The requirements for this patch are included in *Junior Badges and Signs.*

Since Brownie Girl Scouts who are preparing to fly up will usually be doing Bridge to Juniors activities during the last few months of their troop year, Brownie and Junior troops should contact each other during the late winter—informally at leaders' meetings, or by asking your Girl Scout council to link Brownie and Junior troops in convenient locations.

Review the Junior Aide patch activities with the Juniors and talk over the requirements with them. Discuss ways they will be expected to help Brownie Girl Scouts. Share the list of suggested activities for the Bridge to Juniors patch with them so that they will know what the Brownies may be asking them to do. (See page 72 in this leaders' guide.)

Any Number Can Earn It

It is not necessary for an entire troop to assist Brownies. An individual Junior, a patrol, or a Junior Aide interest group may want to earn the patch. Girls wishing to participate will want the assistance of an adult—you, your co-leader, or another troop helper. Encourage girls in their first and second year as Juniors to be Junior Aides. The Brownies who cross the bridge with their help might well be members of their own troop next year.

When Troops Are Linked

Once a Brownie and a Junior troop have been linked, girls and leaders from both troops will need to get together and make plans for bridging activities. After the Brownies have selected their four bridging activities, the Juniors can see where their help will be needed.

As the Junior Aides prepare to assist their younger sister Girl Scouts, you can:

encourage girls to list the parts of program for Juniors that they feel they need to brush up on.

explore with them various ways they might share their knowledge, skill, interests, and enthusiasm with the Brownies. Be an audience if they want to run through an idea or explanation.

help them to anticipate questions Brownies might ask. (What is that badge? What did you do to get it?)

help them to remember how Brownies may feel about the prospect of moving to a new troop and more grown-up activities and responsibilities.

explore with them ways to extend a warm welcome.

give them moral support, showing your confidence in their ability and sensitivity.

Chances are that in doing these things you will learn a lot about how these Juniors feel about their troop, and about some of the ways they have grown and matured.

Brownie Girl Scouts:

Brownie patches recognize participation in activities that an entire troop does together. They encourage cooperative effort, and for the individual girl they stress involvement rather than quality of performance.

	What is Recognized?	Kinds of Opportunities
Brownie B Patches	Participation in total troop activities that focus on the three Brownie B's: Be Discoverers, Be Ready Helpers, Be Friend-Makers.	Involvement in a well-rounded variety of activities; choosing, planning, and carrying out projects.
Bridge to Juniors Patch	Participation with a bridging group in activities that prepare girls to move ahead to Junior Girl Scouting.	Meeting older Girl Scouts; becoming aware of Girl Scouting adventures ahead, feeling welcome in the Junior troop; reviewing Brownie experiences and accomplishments.

Junior Girl Scouts:

Badges and signs recognize an individual girl's completion of specific requirements, either alone or in a group. Earning a badge means developing a skill and sharing it with others. The Junior Aide patch recognizes participation in Brownie-Junior bridging projects.

	What is Recognized?	Kinds of Opportunities
Junior Aide Patch	Active participation in welcoming Brownies who are bridging into Junior Girl Scouting; helping Brownies to learn about, look forward to Junior Girl Scouting.	Teaching, sharing knowledge and skills with younger Girl Scouts; reviewing own experiences and accomplishments.
Junior Badges	Demonstrated growth in knowledge and skills in a specific subject area: successful completion of a specific set of agreed-upon requirements.	Expanding, developing, and using knowledge and skills to help self and others; deciding on ways to accomplish goals; helping to set standards for own accomplishment.
Sign of the Arrow and Sign of the Star	Successful completion of agreed-upon requirements for a series of individual and group projects that focus on a variety of subject areas.	Same as with badges—plus goal setting, developing conscious awareness of own needs, and growth in relation to the four Program Emphases.

Some Guidelines for Measuring Progress

The four Program Emphases, explained on page 9 of this leaders' guide, define the broad objectives of the Girl Scout program. The following charts can help you to look at the progress of girls, as individuals and as a Girl Scout troop, within the field of each Program Emphasis. They can help you to chart the troop's growth and can serve as a basis for setting and reviewing goals. Here's how.

When you begin working with the troop, read through each of these four charts. The items listed under each Emphasis describe a behavior or action you will try to help develop in girls. Try to keep them in mind as you work with the girls throughout the year.

From time to time during the year, look at the charts and put checks in the boxes you feel best describe what is happening in the troop. Look over the charts with your co-leader (and troop consultant, if you have one). Decide together on the areas that need to be worked on, and talk about how to do this. Your job is to try to help girls grow as much and in as many areas as you can.

You might try making different color checks each time you use the charts. In this way, you'll be able to see how much progress has been made. Or you could connect each set of checks with a vertical line and then compare how the connecting lines vary. You'll find that girls may progress in several areas and move backward in another: or things may remain the same for a while. Each troop and each girl is unique and progresses at a different rate. Try to figure out what is (or is not) happening and why.

This is just one way for you to look at the troop's progress. It is meant only to help you. The charts are not to be used by anyone else to judge the troop or its leadership.

	Seldom	Often	Most of the Time
Girls express confidence in their own abilities.			
Girls show interest in trying new things, in meeting new people.			
Activities develop and use the talents and skills of each individual member of the troop.			
Girls initiate ideas.			
Girls are able to decide the "how" as well as the "what" of activities.			
Girls ask for help when they need it, but don't ask adults to plan for them.			
Girls seek information. They want to know the how and why of things that affect them.			

	Seldom	Often	Most of the Time
Girls are willing to tackle and solve problems.			
Girls are comfortable with their decisions.			
Girls are interested in evaluating, in making things work better.			
Girls accept that success or failure of activities depends on their own efforts, not just efforts of others.			
Most activities in the troop come from girls' ideas.			
The troop is able to "make do" and improvise, to have fun without spending a lot of money.			
Girls are known as individuals by their leader(s).			

	Seldom	Often	Most of the Time
Girls get on well together. They have a sense of troop spirit.			
Girls of different ages and school grades develop friendships.			
Girls listen to each other's ideas and concerns.			
Girls help each other, but do not take over each other's jobs.			
Girls enjoy meeting and working with people from a variety of backgrounds.			
The troop has good discussions about problems, and girls figure out solutions.			
If troop rules are needed to guide behavior and interaction, girls help make the rules.			
Girls give support and recognition to each other's efforts, talents, contributions.			

	Seldom	Often	Most of the Time
Group decisions are made democratically, not by just a few girls or by adults.			
Troop officers are good at their jobs and girls respect them.			
Girls are able to make constructive compromises when working with others.			
Girls are able to communicate their feelings and ideas to others.			
Girls are considerate of each other.			
Girls are aware of many of their own strengths and needs for relating comfortably with others.			
There is a feeling of trust and a working partnership among adult and girl members in the troop.			

Emphasis: To help each girl develop values to give meaning and direction to her life.

	Seldom	Often	Most of the Time
Girls express ideas and beliefs freely.			
Girls choose from among a variety of activity/action possibilities.			
Girls show that they think through choices rather than just following the crowd.			
Girls help establish standards for their accomplishment in projects, patches, badges, signs.			
Girls accept responsibility for their own decisions.			
Girls are able to use the Girl Scout Promise and Law as guidelines for their own actions and relationships.			
Girls stand up for what they believe, even if it is not popular.			

	Seldom	Often	Most of the Time
Girls accept their mistakes and are able to grow from them.			
Girls are open to new ways of thinking about and doing things.			
Girls look beyond people's outward behavior and are interested in why people behave or think in certain ways.			
Girls have opportunities to test their values and beliefs by acting on them.			
Girls are able to talk about things that are important to them right now.			
Girls are able to look ahead to future roles as women in their society.			
Girls question their adult leader's decisions and actions when they don't agree with them.			

Emphasis: To help each girl contribute to her society through her own talents and in cooperative efforts with others.

	Seldom	Often	Most of the Time
Girls are able to identify what they can do together for the good of all—in their own troop or home and in their community.			
Girls are prepared to be useful in emergencies.			
Girls show interest in learning about the customs and traditions of various groups and cultures.			
Girls have been places and have interacted with people outside their own town or neighborhood.			
Girls show their concern about protecting their environment by doing something about it.			
Girls decide on their own to do things for people around them.			
When they plan to help others, girls are able to identify the skills they need to do a good job.			

	Seldom	Often	Most of the Time
Girls like to help others and can help by doing *with* rather than for.			
Girls are able to think of creative and realistic ways to help where needed.			
Girls consider the talents and abilities of troop members when making plans for activities.			
Troop government functions well in the troop.			
Girls can organize together for carrying their plans into action.			
Girls are aware of how their community is organized and how various community services are provided.			
Girls are able to make contacts with resource people to help with their troop's activities.			
Girls reach out for increasing responsibility in running their troop.			

Worlds to Explore: Resources

To supplement this book and the girls' handbook, look for resources in Girl Scout catalogs of publications and audiovisuals; also in your public library.

The following list is just a sampling of the many, many materials that can be helpful to you as a Brownie or Junior Girl Scout leader. Specific aspects of your job that relate to each item are indicated by letters under the entries. The letter code is:

L

leadership techniques; relating to girls

G

Girl Scout history, traditions, ways of work

W

World of Well-Being

P

World of People

T

World of Today and Tomorrow

A

World of the Arts

O

World of the Out-of-Doors

Resources with an asterisk (*) are available by mail order only. Send your order to the address nearest you:

Girl Scouts of the U.S.A.
National Equipment Service

East: 830 Third Avenue
   New York, N.Y. 10022

West & Midwest: P.O. Box 1400
          St. Louis, Mo. 63188

Order audiovisual materials direct from:
Girl Scouts of the U.S.A.
Girl Scout Film Library
830 Third Avenue
New York, N.Y. 10022

Girl Scout Resources—Books

Basics. Cat. No. 23-961, 50¢. 1976. Published by the World Association of Girl Guides and Girl Scouts. Written for the leader, it gives some history of the World Association; for example, its composition, object, membership structure, and finance. The appendices include lists of World Conferences, member organizations, and addresses of world centers.

L   G   P

Be an EQ Traveler. Margaret Olsen. Cat. No. 19-966, 25¢. 1971. Delightfully illustrated pocketbook of environmental hints for groups on the move.

O

The Beginner's Cookbook.* Jody Cameron Malis. Cat. No. 26-114, 95¢. 1972. Published for GSUSA by Dell Publishing Co. Introduction to cooking for ages 7-12.

W

Brownies' Own Songbook. Cat. No. 23-130, $1.50. 1968. 45 favorite singing games and action songs with instructions especially suited to 6, 7, 8 year-olds. To use with girls.

P   A   O

Cooking Out-of-Doors. Cat. No. 19-984, $3.25. 1960. Outdoor cooking for novice to experienced camper with 250 recipes keyed to ingredients, skill levels, and method of cooking.

W   O

Daisy Low of the Girl Scouts. Cat. No. 19-991, 25¢. 1975. Colorful comic book version of the story of Juliette Low.

G

Eco-Antics. Mabel Hammersmith and Laura Watkins. Cat. No. 19-989, $1.25. 1974. Action-oriented projects designed to help girls gain an understanding of their environment.

O

Exploring the Hand Arts. Corinne Murphy. Cat. No. 19-304, $2.25. 1955. Projects and design suggestions in many media.

P A ©

Feeding A Crowd. Judy Cook. Cat. No. 19-977, 35¢. 1973. Guidelines for planning, organizing, and managing meals for large groups; quantity recipes and shopping tips.

W ©

Games for Girl Scouts. Joan McEniry. Cat. No. 20-630, $1.50. 1969. Excellent collection of many kinds and varieties of games for indoors and out.

W P ©

"GSUSA Program Standards," pages 87-91 in this leader's guide. Information about Girl Scout program standards and their application to troop activities.

L

The Great Cookie Caper Or, How To Discover The World Starting With A Cookie Or Anything Else. Cat. No. 19-150, 35¢. 1973. For young Brownies and leaders. Play-filled activities and ideas designed to stimulate curiosity, creativity, and desire to learn.

L W A ©

Guide Games and Recipes. Cat. No. 23-946, 50¢. 1967. Produced by WAGGGS.

P W

Happily Appley—A Leader's Guide to Food Fun with Young Children. Elizabeth Munz. Cat. No. 19-995, $2.50. 1975. Food-related activities to help younger Girl Scouts develop good eating habits.

W P A ©

Hiking—In Town or Country.* Catharine C. Reiley. Cat. No. 26-339, $1.00. 1952. All about hiking, with ideas on what to do along the way.

©

Juliette Low and the Girl Scouts. Cat. No. 19-409, $1.75. 1960. Official biography of Juliette Gordon Low.

G

Leader's Digest.* Cat. No. 26-131, 25¢. 1976. Information on the beliefs and policies of Girl Scouts of the U.S.A.

L G

Let's Take A Walk—An Activity Picture Book with Group Leader's Guide. Cat. No. 19-992, $1.75. 1975. Picture-story activity book for children ages 5-8 uses a walk around the neighborhood as the starting point for wide-ranging activities usable in every environment. Stresses use of senses as tools for discovery.

L A ©

Littlest Girl Scout, The: A Leadership Guide for Working with the Young Child. Cat. No. 19-997, 75¢. 1975. Information for councils and leaders in working with the youngest girls in Girl Scouting.

L

Map of WAGGGS Countries.* Cat. No. 26-110, 100 for $2.50. 1973. For all Girl Scouts and Girl Guides. Illustrations identify 11 girls in uniforms of other countries. World map with keyed list of WAGGGS members.

G P

Me And My Dog—An Activity Picture Book with Group Leader's Guide. Cat. No. 19-996, $1.75. 1975. A story about a little girl and her dog. For beginning readers.

L

Our Songs. Cat. No. 23-465, 80¢. 1942. The basic songbook for Brownies. Simple but delightful songs.

P A ©

Planning Trips with Girl Scouts. Cat. No. 19-998, $1.25. 1977. Step-by-step progression in planning group travel from day hikes to overnight trips.

L P ©

Safety-Wise. Cat. No. 26-205, 75¢. 1977. For adults who work with girls. Basic health and safety practices for all Girl Scout activities. Program and Camping Standards. Sample charts, forms, applications, permissions, health examinations.

L W ©

Sing Together—A Girl Scout Songbook. Cat. No. 20-206, $2.50. 1973. Songs for almost every occasion. Includes traditional folk songs from several countries as well as blues, jazz, and contemporary.

P A ©

Sing Together Sampler.* Cat. No. 26-811, $4.00. 1974. 2- track, 40-minute cassette teaching aid to use with **Sing Together.** For the adult who needs to hear the songs before teaching, to use with girls, or just listen to for enjoyment.

L P A ©

Standard First Aid & Personal Safety.* Cat. No. 26-255, $1.95. 1973. Published for The American National Red Cross by Doubleday & Co. Instructional text for leaders and Juniors of how-to's for personal safety, emergency first aid, and accident prevention.

L W ©

Trefoil Round the World. Cat. No 23-962, $2.50. Updated 1975. Produced by WAGGGS. Information on Girl Guide and Girl Scout associations around the world.

L G P

Troop Camping. Betty Gene Alley. Cat. No. 19-515, 25¢. 1971. Details how to find a campsite and resources; equipment; preparation.

©

Troop Records and Reports (complete set with ring binder). Cat. No. 21-292, $3.00.

L G

Unravel The World—A Resources Bibliography for Global Understanding.* Cat. No. 26-702, 50¢. 1975. Bibliography of resources, people, books, audiovisuals, and community organizations for international activities and projects.

W P A

Girl Scout Resources—Audiovisuals

Because of Camping.* AV 13-62, $15.00. 1967. 35 mm, color, 110 frames.
◎

Flipcharts on Camping Skills*:
Compass and Maps. AV 15-04, $10.00. 1973.
Ⅼ   ◎

Fire Building. AV 15-02, $10.00. 1973.
Ⅼ   ◎

Knots and Lashing. AV 15-01, $10.00. 1973.
Ⅼ   ◎

Primitive Camp Sanitation. AV 15-03, $10.00. 1974.
Ⅼ   ◎

Tents and Simple Shelters. AV 15-06, $10.00. 1973.
Ⅼ   ◎

Toolcraft. AV 15-0 5, $10.00. 1973.
Ⅼ   ◎

Also available as pocketbooks from NES:
Compass and Maps. Cat. No. 26-210. 1976.
Fire Building. Cat. No. 26-212. 1976.
Knots and Lashing. Cat. No. 26-213. 1976.
Primitive Camp Sanitation. Cat. No. 26-215. 1976.
Tents and Simple Shelters. Cat. No. 26-211. 1976.
Toolcraft. Cat. No. 26-214. 1976.

Pots and Plots in Lots of Spots.* AV 13-92, $15.00. 1975. 35 mm, color. Demonstrates the achievements possible when young children are inspired to beautify sites in their neighborhoods. Original art and music.
Ⓟ   ◎

Girl Scout Resources—Magazines

Daisy magazine. Monthly, October through June, for Brownies and Juniors. Happenings in Girl Scouting and Girl Guiding around the world; games, stories, information, and action projects; opportunities for individual and troop participation. Content geared to troop year; supports all aspects of Girl Scout program. Subscription information on troop registration form (bottom copy) and in **Girl Scout Leader** magazine; or write to Magazine Department, Girl Scouts of the U.S.A., 830 Third Avenue, New York, N.Y. 10022.
Ⓖ   Ⓦ   Ⓟ   Ⓣ   Ⓐ   ◎

Girl Scout Leader magazine. Current and future happenings in Girl Scouting, practical tips on leadership of girls, inspiration and encouragement.
Ⓛ   Ⓖ   Ⓦ   Ⓟ   Ⓣ   Ⓐ   ◎

Resources of Other Publishers

Adkins, Jan. **Toolchest: A Primer of Woodcraft.** New York: Walker & Co., 1973. A beautiful, interesting, and well-illustrated book on the tools of woodworking. Written for young people.
Ⓣ   Ⓐ

Alexander, Marthann. **Weaving on Cardboard: Simple Looms to Make and Use.** New York: Taplinger Publishing Co., Inc., 1972. Additional ideas for using the cardboard loom described in Worlds to Explore handbook. To use with girls.
Ⓟ   Ⓣ   Ⓐ   ◎

Allison, Linda. **The Reasons for Seasons: The Great Cosmic Megagalactic Trip Without Moving from Your Chair.** Boston: Little, Brown & Co., 1975. Things to do, things to make, and ideas to think about related to the earth and sky, all arranged according to the seasons.
◎

Arizona Cactus-Pine Girl Scout Council, Inc. **Arizona Heritage Cookbook.** 1975. Order from Arizona Cactus-Pine Girl Scout Council, 1515 East Osborn Road, Phoenix, Arizona 85014. $3.50 plus 50¢ for postage and handling.
Ⓦ   Ⓟ   ◎

Aylesworth, Thomas G., ed. **It Works Like This: A Collection of Machines from Nature and Science Magazine.** Garden City, N.Y.: Natural History Press, 1968.
Ⓣ

Bambra, Audrey and Webster, Muriel. **Teaching Folk Dancing.** New York: Theatre Arts Books, 1972. Additional folk dances to supplement those in girls' book, with good instruction for teaching.
Ⓛ   Ⓟ   Ⓐ   ◎

Beaney, Jan. **Adventures with Collage.** New York: Frederick Warne & Co., Inc., 1970. To use with girls.
Ⓐ   ◎

Belves, Pierre and Mathey, Francois. **Enjoying the World of Art.** New York: Lion Press, 1966. Written for young people.

————.**How Artists Work.** New York: Lion Press, 1968. Written for young people. Simple explanations of how art works in several media.
Ⓐ

Bendick, Jeanne. **Place to Live: A Study of Ecology.** New York: Parents Magazine Press, 1970.
◎

Bendick, Jeanne and Bendick, Robert. **Filming Works Like This.** New York: McGraw-Hill Book Co., 1971.
Ⓣ   Ⓐ

Bernikow, Louise, ed. **The World Split Open: Four Centuries of Women Poets in England and America 1552-1950.** New York: Random House, Inc., 1974. Nice collection to help appreciate some fine poetry often not included in other anthologies.

ℙ 𝔸

Blake, Jim and Ernst, Barbara. **The Great Perpetual Learning Machine.** Boston: Little, Brown & Co., 1976. A collection of activities and resources for use with children in subjects related to all of the Worlds. Includes projects, games, and guides for further exploration; many pictures and diagrams. An excellent resource book attractively organized.

𝕎 ℙ 𝕋 𝔸 ◎

Bley, Edgar S. **Best Singing Games for Children of All Ages.** New York: Sterling Publishing Co., Inc., 1959. Good selection of simple singing games.

𝕎 ℙ 𝔸 ◎

Borten, Helen. **Do You Move As I Do.** (Picture Book Series) New York: Abelard-Schuman Ltd., 1963.

_____. **Do You See What I See.** (Picture Book Series) New York: Abelard-Schuman Ltd., 1959. Books for leaders and girls to use together for understanding movement, dance, and visual appreciation of the arts.

𝕎 𝔸

Brandon, William, ed. **Magic World: American Indian Songs and Poems.** New York: William Morrow & Co., Inc., 1972.

ℙ 𝔸

Busch, Phyllis. **Puddles and Ponds: Living Things in Watery Places.** Cleveland, Ohio: William Collins & World Publishing, Co., Inc., 1969. The explanation of ecosystems, communities, and habitats.

◎

Cannon, Calvin and Wickens, Elaine. **What I Like To Do.** New York: Coward, McCann & Geoghegan, Inc., 1971. Written for children.

𝕎

Castellini, John. **Rudiments of Music.** New York: W. W. Norton & Co., Inc., 1962. Basic help to understanding notation and harmony. For leader to use and interpret to girls.

𝕃 𝔸

Castino, Ruth and Pickens, Marjorie. **Spinning and Dyeing the Natural Way.** New York: Van Nostrand Reinhold Co., 1974.

𝔸 ◎

Clark, Ann N. **The Little Indian Basket Maker.** Chicago: Melmont Publishers, Inc., 1957. A book for girls to read and enjoy for appreciation of the arts of North American Indian.

ℙ 𝔸 ◎

Cobb, Vicki. **How the Doctor Knows You're Fine.** Philadelphia: J. B. Lippincott Co., 1973. Written for children.

_____. **Science Experiments You Can Eat.** Philadelphia: J. B. Lippincott Co., 1972.

𝕎 𝕋

Cooper, Terry T. and Ratner, Marilyn. **Many Hands Cooking: An International Cookbook for Girls and Boys.** New York: Thomas Y. Crowell Co., 1974.

𝕎 ℙ

De Bono, Edward. **Children Solve Problems.** New York: Harper & Row Publishers, Inc., 1974.

𝕃

Deutsch, Ronald. **Family Guide to Better Food and Better Health.** Des Moines, Iowa: Creative Home Library, 1971.

𝕎

Devlin, Harry. **What Kind of a House Is That.** New York: Parents Magazine Press, 1969. Simple, readable, and visually attractive book to help in understanding styles of architecture. Written for young people.

𝕋 𝔸 ◎

Enthoven, Jacqueline. **Stitchery for Children: A Manual for Teachers, Parents, and Children.** New York: Van Nostrand Reinhold Co., 1968.

𝔸

Festival Figures. Set of 14″-tall cardboard figures (4 boys, 4 girls) in full-color festival attire of eight countries: Ecuador, Iran, Kenya, Lebanon, Nigeria, Pakistan, Panama, and the Philippines. Information on the clothing of each country is included. For educational and decorative uses. Order from: U.S. Committee for UNICEF, 331 East 38th Street, New York, N.Y. 10016. No. 5009, $2.00.

ℙ

Freed, Alvyn M. **T. A. for Kids (and Grown-Ups Too).** Sacramento, Calif.: Jalmar Press, Inc., 1971. Simple self-awareness exercises to do with girls.

𝕃 𝕎

Gieg, John P. and Blair, John G. **There Is A Difference.** Washington, D.C.: Meridian House International. Twelve intercultural perspectives which help us to become aware of and to identify the differences in thought patterns, life styles, and goals of people from around the world.

ℙ

Golden Guides Series (includes **Golden Field Guides, Golden Nature Guides, Golden Science Guides**). New York: Western Publishing Co., Inc. Good for identification and basic information on rocks, stars, trees, nature, animals, etc.

𝕋 ◎

Goodwin, Mary T. and Pollen, Gerry. **Creative Food Experiences for Children.** Washington, D.C.: Day Care & Child Development Council of America, Inc., 1974. Program ideas based on nutrition education. Order from: Center for Science in the Public Interest, 1779 Church Street, N.W., Washington, D.C. 20036.

𝕎

Gordon, Thomas, M.D. **Parent Effectiveness Training: The Tested New Way to Raise Responsible Children.** New York: David McKay Co., Inc., 1970. Ideas and methods for working effectively with children.

𝕃

Guild, Vera P. **Painting with Stitches: A Guide to Embroidery, Needlepoint, Crochet and Macrame.** Worcester, Mass.: Davis Publications, Inc., 1976.

A

Hallamore, Elisabeth. **The Metric Book of Amusing Things To Do.** Woodbury, N.Y.: Barron's Educational Series, Inc., 1975. An easy and fun way to enjoy as well as learn metrics. For adults and girls.

T

Hallock, Constance M. **Fun and Festival from Southeast Asia.** New York: Friendship Press, 1968. Games, songs, food, dress, and program ideas. Particularly good for children ages 7-12. Order from: Friendship Press, Room 772, 475 Riverside Drive, New York, N.Y. 10027. $1.25.

P

Hammett, Catherine T. **Your Own Book of Campcraft.** New York: Pocket Books, Inc., 1971. Everything you need to know about campcraft skills and philosophy in pocketbook size.

◎

Hofsinde, Robert. **Indian Arts.** New York: William Morrow & Co., Inc., 1971.

P A

How to Make and Use a Pinhole Camera. Purchase at your local photo dealer or order from: Eastman Kodak Company, Consumer Markets Division, Rochester, N.Y. 14650. Publication No. AA-5., 15¢. For other publications on photography contact your local photo dealer.

T ◎

Hunt, B. **Complete How-to Book of Indian Craft.** (Original title: Ben Hunt's Big Indiancraft Book.) New York: Macmillan Publishing Co., Inc., 1973.

P A ◎

Hunt, Sarah E. **Games and Sports the World Around.** New York: Ronald Press Co., 1964.

W P ◎

Ickis, Marguerite. **The Book of Festivals and Holidays the World Over.** New York: Dodd, Mead & Co., 1970.

W P

Janson, Horst W. and Janson, Dora J. **The Story of Painting for Young People.** New York: Harry N. Abrams, Inc., 1962.

A

Joseph, Joan. **Folk Toys Around the World and How To Make Them.** New York: Parents Magazine Press, 1972. Several simple examples of toys from several countries. Good to use with girls.

W P A ◎

Kepple, Ella H. **Fun and Festival from Latin America.** New York: Friendship Press, 1961. Games, songs, food, dress, and program ideas. Particularly good for children ages 7-12. Order from: Friendship Press, Room 772, 475 Riverside Drive, New York, N.Y. 10027. $1.25.

P

Kimball, Richard L. **Making Small Things Look Bigger.** San Leandro, Calif.: Educational Science Consultants, 1971.

T

Knopf, Mildred O. **Mildred O. Knopf's Around The World Cookbook for Young People.** New York: Alfred A. Knopf, Inc., 1966.

W P

Kupferberg, Herbert. **A Rainbow of Sound.** New York: Charles Scribner's Sons, 1973. An excellent book exploring instruments of the orchestra and their music. Good to use with girls.

A

Landeck, Beatrice. **More Songs to Grow On.** New York: William Morrow & Co., Inc., 1954. An excellent song book for Brownies and young Juniors.

A

Larrick, Nancy. **A Parent's Guide to Children's Reading.** New York: Doubleday & Co., Inc., 1975. For adults. This is an excellent resource and guide to help girls choose worthwhile books to read and enjoy. Updated every year.

L A

Lawson, John D., et al. **Leadership Is Everybody's Business: A Practical Guide for Volunteer Membership Groups.** San Luis Obispo, Calif.: Impact Publishers, Inc., 1976. A useful, readable, practical, and entertaining book. It provides step-by-step guides for learning leadership behavior and developing group techniques that lead to group solidarity, creativity, positive and effective action, and the satisfaction of achievement.

L

Le Shan, Eda. **What Makes Me Feel This Way?** New York: Macmillan Publishing Co., Inc., 1972.

W

Lidston, John and McIntosh, Don. **Children as Film Makers.** New York: Van Nostrand Reinhold Co., 1976.

T A

Macaulay, David. **Underground.** Boston: Houghton Mifflin Co., 1976. Excellent pictorial book written for young people to show what structures are unseen under the ground in towns and cities.

T A ◎

McGuire, Leslie. **You, How Your Body Works.** New York: Platt & Munk Publishers, 1974.

W

Medsger, Betty. **Women At Work.** Mission, Kans.: Sheed Andrews & McMeel, Inc., 1975.

W T

Meyer, Carolyn. **Saw, Hammer, and Paint: Woodworking and Finishing for Beginners.** New York: William Morrow & Co., Inc., 1973. Basics on using woodworking tools and finishing projects.

T A ◎

Meyer, Jerome S. **Boiling Water in a Paper Cup and Other Unbelievables.** New York: Scholastic Book Services, 1973.

New Games Foundation. **The New Games Book.** Ed. by Andrew Fluegelman. New York: Doubleday & Co., Inc., 1976.

OBIS (Outdoor Biological Instructive Strategies) **Module Trail Kit, Kit #1, Kit #2, Kit #3,** Lawrence Hall of Science, Berkeley, Calif. 94720. An informative series of nature experiences for your girls and yourself. An exciting program to pursue.

Paine, Roberta M. **Looking at Architecture.** New York: Lothrop, Lee & Shepard Co., 1974. Beautiful book, written for young people, outlines various styles of architecture and how to understand and appreciate their structure.

Pettit, Florence H. **How to Make Whirligigs & Whimmy Diddles and Other American Folkcraft Objects.** New York: Thomas Y. Crowell Co., 1972. An excellent book with many authentic folk arts of the U.S.A., with good instructions on how to make them.

Rainey, Sarita. **Weaving Without a Loom.** Worcester, Mass.: Davis Publications, Inc., 1966. Next step after the simple beginning of cardboard loom in handbook. Several excellent examples without costly looms.

Rey, H. A. **Find the Constellations.** rev. ed. Boston: Houghton Mifflin Co., 1976.

_____. **The Stars: A New Way to See Them.** Boston: Houghton Mifflin Co., 1976. Clear, stimulating, and often humorous books on constellations and the stars written for young children. Both books contain sky charts and time tables.

Rieger, Shay. **Animals in Clay.** New York: Charles Scribner's Sons, 1971. Good, basic book for working in clay for first experiences.

Ross, Russell. **A Teacher's Guide to Ten-Minute Field Trips Using the School Grounds for Environmental Studies.** Illinois: J. C. Ferguson Publishing Co., 1973.

Rowland, Joan. **Fun and Festival from the Middle East.** New York: Friendship Press, 1970. Games, songs, food, dress, and program ideas. Particularly good for children ages 7-12. Order from: Friendship Press, Room 772, 475 Riverside Drive, New York, N.Y. 10027. $1.25.

Samson, Joan. **Watching the New Baby.** New York: Atheneum Publishers, 1974. Written for children.

Sanders, Lisbeth P. **Fit For Fun.** Chicago: American Medical Association, 1969. Written for children.

Schachner, Erwin. **Printmaking, Step by Step.** New York: Western Publishing Co., Inc., 1970. Good, basic book on several methods of creating prints, expanding horizons from those in handbook.

Shalit, Nathan. **Cup and Saucer Chemistry.** New York: Grosset & Dunlap, Inc., 1974. Simple experiments that can be accomplished in a kitchen. (grades 3-6)

Simon, Sidney B. **I Am Loveable and Capable.** Niles, Ill.: Argus Communications, 1974. Simple presentation of human relations. Adaptable for use with girls.

_____.et al. **Values Clarification: A Handbook of Practical Strategies For Teachers and Students.** New York: Hart Publishing Co., 1972. Does not teach a particular set of values, but presents numerous activities that help people to examine and formulate their own value systems.

Skelsey, Alice and Huckaby, Gloria. **Growing Up Green.** New York: Workman Publishing Co., Inc., 1973. Written for adults, the book is packed with ideas and action ways to introduce young children to the world around them.

Thomas, Marlo, et al. **Free To Be...You and Me.** New York: McGraw-Hill Book Co., 1974.

Untermeyer, Louis. **Tales from the Ballet.** New York: Western Publishing Co., Inc., 1968. An excellent book for young people to increase enjoyment and appreciation of the most familiar ballets.

Van Matre, Steve. **Acclimatization.** Martinsville, Ind.: American Camping Association, 1972. A sensory and conceptual approach to the natural environment.

_____. **Acclimatizing.** Martinsville, Ind.: American Camping Association, 1974. Activity models for total involvement.

Vinton, I. **The Folkways Omnibus of Children's Games.** New York: Hawthorn Books, Inc., 1974. Games for all ages from all over the world. Background material on games is included.

Vocational-Technical Curriculum Laboratory. **Technology for Children.** 1974. Bldg. 4103, Kilmer Campus, Rutgers—The State University, New Brunswick, N.J. 08903.

Ward, Winifred. **Stories to Dramatize.** Anchorage, Ky.: Anchorage Press, 1952. An excellent resource for continuing with dramatic activities.

Watts, May T. **Flower Finder: A Manual for Identifying Spring Wildflowers and Flower Families East of Rockies.** Berkeley, Calif.: Nature Study Guild, 1955.

_____. **Master Tree Finder: A Manual for Identifying Trees by Their Leaves East of Rockies.** Berkeley, Calif.: Nature Study Guild, 1963.

_____. **Reading the Landscape of America.** rev. ed. New York: Macmillan Publishing Co., Inc., 1975. The effect of man and nature on land patterns. Available in both hardcover and paperback.

_____. **Tree Finder: A Simplified Manual for Identifying Common Trees East of Rockies.** Berkeley, Calif.: Nature Study Guild, 1963.
©

Watts, May T. and Watts, Tom. **Desert Tree Finder: A Manual for Identifying Desert Trees of Arizona, California, New Mexico.** Berkeley, Calif.: Nature Study Guild, 1974.

_____. **Winter Tree Finder: A Manual for Identifying Deciduous Trees in Winter East of Rockies.** Berkeley, Calif.: Nature Study Guild, 1970.
©

Watts, Tom. **Pacific Coast Tree Finder: A Manual for Identifying Pacific Coast Trees.** Berkeley, Calif.: Nature Study Guild, 1973.

_____. **Rocky Mountain Tree Finder: A Manual for Identifying Rocky Mountain Trees.** Berkeley, Calif.: Nature Study Guild, 1972.

Pocketbooks on how to identify flowers, trees, and desert plants by their leaves or flower parts.
©

Weiss, Harvey. **Ceramics, from Clay to Kiln.** Reading, Mass.: Addison-Wesley Publishing Co., Inc., 1964.

_____. **Collage and Construction.** Reading, Mass.: Addison-Wesley Publishing Co., Inc., 1970.

_____. **Lens and Shutter.** Reading, Mass.: Addison-Wesley Publishing Co., Inc., 1971.

_____. **Paint, Brush and Palette.** Reading, Mass.: Addison-Wesley Publishing Co., Inc., 1966.

_____. **Paint, Ink and Roller.** Reading, Mass.: Addison-Wesley Publishing Co., Inc., 1958.

All five are excellent resources on the subjects listed. Clear, simple text, good illustrations foster appreciation as well as technique.
T   A   ©

_____. **Pencil, Pen and Brush.** New York: Scholastic Book Services, 1974. Drawing and graphics skills. Excellent resource.
A

_____. **Gadget Book.** New York: Thomas Y. Crowell Co., 1971. 24 gadgets to make from simple materials to inspire young people to tinker.
T

_____. **How to Make Your Own Books.** New York: Thomas Y. Crowell Co., 1974. Clear and simple text. How to cover and bind personalized books.
A

_____. **Model Airplanes and How to Build Them.** New York: Thomas Y. Crowell Co., 1975. Fantasy machines are starting points for imagination.
T   A

_____. **Model Cars and Trucks and How to Build Them.** New York: Thomas Y. Crowell, Co., 1974. Good, simple how-to's for designing and constructing all sorts of vehicles on wheels.
T   A

_____. **Motors and Engines and How They Work.** New York: Thomas Y. Crowell, Co., 1969. How to make electric, water, wind, gravity, and spring powered motors.
T

_____. **Ship Models and How to Build Them.** New York: Thomas Y. Crowell, Co., 1973. Every step of creating wide range of boats from tub-boats to hollow-hulled schooners.
T   A

Wigginton, Eliot, ed. **Foxfire Two.** New York: Doubleday & Co., Inc., 1975. Several folk arts of Appalachian region with narrative report of life of people who create the arts.
P   A   ©

Williams, Oscar, ed. **The Pocket Book of Modern Verse.** New York: Washington Square Press, Inc., 1972. A good, comprehensive collection suitable for just enjoyment and finding poetry for wide variety of occasions and ceremonies.
A

Wright, Rose. **Fun and Festival from Africa.** New York: Friendship Press, 1967. Games, songs, food, dress, and program ideas. Particularly good for children ages 7-12. Order from: Friendship Press, Room 772, 475 Riverside Drive, New York, N.Y. 10027. $1.25.
P

Yurchenco, Henrietta. **Fiesta of Folk Songs of Spain and Latin America.** New York: G. P. Putnam's Sons, 1967.
P   A

Magazines

The Curious Naturalist. Beautiful publication of facts and discovery activities about the natural world for people of all ages. Issued four times a year by Massachusetts Audubon Society, Lincoln, Mass. 01773.

Eco-News. Environmental newsletter for young people. Published ten times a year by Environmental Action Coalition, Inc., 233 East 49th Street, New York, N.Y. 10017.

Learning magazine. Education Today Company, Inc., 530 University Avenue, Palo Alto, Calif. 94301. Creative learning ideas for the classroom, many of which can be adapted to a troop situation.

National Geographic World. Monthly magazine of information and activities on the environment, people, and places for the 6 to 11 year-old. Published by National Geographic Society, 17th and M Streets N.W., Washington, D.C. 20036.

Ranger Rick. Magazine of games, stories and environmental awareness for the 6 to 11 year-old. Published by National Wildlife Federation, 1412 16th Street N.W., Washington, D.C. 20036.

Organizations

Amateur Athletic Union of U.S., 3400 West 86th Street, Indianapolis, Ind. 46268. Physical fitness tests available with instructions and scoring sheets. Awards also available for any girl 8-10 achieving the desired level of fitness. Small charge to cover cost of mailing and processing awards.

American National Red Cross. Contact local chapter for pamphlets, posters, information on first aid, safety, swimming and small craft courses, textbooks, and program ideas. Pamphlets and posters are usually distributed at no cost. Books, however, must be purchased.

Child Study Association Press, 50 Madison Avenue, New York, N.Y. 10010. Good source of book lists appropriate for girls of this age.

Garden Club of America, 598 Madison Avenue, New York, N.Y. 10022. Write for free packet of material on gardening and conservation for Girl Scout troop leaders.

International Book Project, 17 Mentelle Park, Lexington, Ky. 40502. Send your name and address for an assignment: a person or family in another country with whom you can share books and magazines.

IFOFSAG Stamp Bank, The Stamp Bank, Box 104, 1601 Fredrikstad, Norway. Used stamps from the United States or other countries that are sent to the Stamp Bank are credited as cash to a Development Fund. This fund assists development work in Girl Guide/ Boy Scout associations throughout the world. The Bank welcomes all stamps, on or off paper, that are not torn, thinned, stained, or missing perforation. Arrange stamps face up in plastic bags and then pack in a box. Mark the outside of the box "Used Postage Stamps" so it will enter Norway duty free.

National Audubon Society, 950 Third Avenue, New York, N.Y. 10022. Write for catalog of free and inexpensive nature publications.

National Safety Council, Youth Department, 425 N. Michigan Avenue, Chicago, Ill. 60611. Magazines, pamphlets, posters, program ideas, and materials on many aspects of safety including bicycle safety, home safety, swimming safety, etc. The Youth Department also conducts an awards program recognizing group or individual safety projects.

National Wildlife Association, 1412 10th Street N.W., Washington, D.C. 20030. Write for free catalogs of conservation education publications.

New Eyes for the Needy, Inc., 549 Millburn Avenue, Short Hills, N.J. 07078. Send discarded eyeglasses and odd bits of jewelry to the above address. These are redeemed by the organization for cash and, in turn, used to send eyeglasses to hospitals and welfare agencies as requested in Africa, Asia, and Latin America.

U.S. Committee for UNICEF, 331 East 38th Street, New York, N.Y. 10016. A gold mine of inexpensive publications, materials and resource information. Write for catalog.

U.S. Department of Agriculture, Agricultural Research Service, Office of Communications, Washington, D.C. 20250. Pamphlets on nutrition and safe food preparation and storage, camping, conservation, and gardening. Send for list of publications.

U.S. Department of the Interior, Interior Building, between 18th & 19th Streets N.W., Washington, D.C. 20240. Write to Directors of Information of Bureau of Outdoor Recreation, Bureau of Land Management, and National Park Service for listings of free and inexpensive material.

Girl Scout Program Standards

"The Girl Scout program is an informal educational program designed to help girls put into practice the fundamental principles of the Girl Scout movement as set forth in the Preamble [to the Constitution]. It is carried out in small groups with adult leadership and provides a wide range of activities developed around the interests and needs of girls."

Constitution of Girl Scouts of the United States of America, Article III

All Girl Scout program is based on the Promise and Law. These program standards, established by the national organization, are guides for councils and troops in judging and improving the quality of program for girls. They are intended to help leaders by indicating practices which experience has shown to be safe and effective. They amplify and interpret the policies in the *Blue Book of Basic Documents.* For health and safety concerns the book, *Safety-Wise*, should be followed.

A standard is something established by authority, custom, or general consent as a criterion for a given purpose. Standards are similar to policies in that they help people to achieve effective results through consistent action. Standards differ from policies in that they are models, rather than strict rules, for action. Standards are more flexibly worded than policies. This permits people to exercise a certain degree of judgment in order to meet the needs of a particular situation.

Adult Leadership

(See also the "Leadership" section in *Safety-Wise*.)

1 Each Brownie, Junior, and Cadette troop should have an adult ("adult" as defined by state statute) leader and an assistant leader. Each Senior troop should have an adult adviser.

2 Leaders/advisers should follow recognized health and safety procedures. The leader or other responsible adult designated by her (e.g., a program consultant) should be present during troop meetings and/or related small-group activities.

3 At least two adults should accompany girls when they are troop camping, on other special trips, or attending an event. The following ratios of girls to adults should be used as guides for such activities:

Ratio of Girls to Adults

Two adults to every:

| 12 Brownies |
| 16 Juniors |
| 24 Cadettes |

One adult to each additional:

| 6 Brownies |
| 8 Juniors |
| 12 Cadettes |

When girls of any age level are involved in activities of unusual risk, the number of adults accompanying them should depend on the nature of the activity, the site, the size of the group, and the maturity of the girls (see *Safety-Wise*, camping standard 84). These same criteria should be used to determine the number of adults accompanying Senior Girl Scouts (see *Safety-Wise*, camping standard 77).

4 Each troop should have an active troop committee of registered adult members who provide support and continuity to the troop. The troop leader/adviser should help find members for the troop committee and keep them informed about the troop plans.

5 A member of the troop's sponsoring group should be included on the troop committee.

6 Program consultants for activities should be selected on these bases:
 technical competence and ability to share specialized skills,
 willingness to follow Girl Scout program and ways of work,
 willingness to cooperate with the leader in carrying out the project.

7 Every troop leader/adviser should take advantage of basic and advanced program, training, or adult education opportunities provided by the council or outside organizations.

Troop Organization

(See also the "Site" section in *Safety-Wise*.)

8 Troops should include girls from more than one school grade and should reflect the diversity of socio-economic, racial, cultural, and religious groups in the community.

9 Troops should be small enough to allow for development of the individual girl, but large enough to give the group experience in self-government. Patrols, where used, should not exceed eight girls apiece.

10 Troops should meet often enough to fulfill the needs and interests of girls and to maintain continuity. Scheduled events, safety concerns, and availability of transportation and meeting places should be considered when planning meeting times. Generally the meetings are scheduled as follows:

Brownies	once a week for one to two hours
Juniors	once a week for one to two hours
Cadettes	once a week or as decided by the girls and their leader
Seniors	regularly as decided by the girls with their adviser

11 Troops should meet in places that are easily accessible to all members and that provide the following:

safe, clean, well-ventilated, well-heated space, free from hazards;

area large enough for active games and small-group meetings;

first aid equipment;

toilets with handwashing facilities;

storage space;

access to telephone.

12 Sites for large groups of girls, three troops or more, should meet the same standards as those for troop meeting places and should also have enough room and facilities to prevent crowding and sufficient, operational, well-marked emergency exits.

13 Leaders/advisers and girls should respect the opinions and practices of all religious, ethnic, racial, linguistic, and socio-economic groups in the troop membership when:

choosing meeting places,

selecting meeting dates and times,

planning group activities,

considering schedules for trips,

making group menus.

14 Special consideration should be given to the needs of handicapped girls when selecting meeting places and planning activities. See *Safety-Wise*, camping standards 124 and 126.

15 Leaders/advisers should provide girls with the necessary information and assistance to move from one age level to the next in Girl Scouting. Councils should provide opportunities for girls to transfer from one troop to another, within or outside the council, and to enter at the appropriate age level.

16 Credit should be given for continuity of membership and for badge requirements and other activities (when properly recorded) to girls who have been affiliated with recognized Girl Scout/Girl Guide movements in other countries.

Program Activities

17 The program should be based on the needs and interests of girls and include opportunities for:

a wide variety of activities,

individual and group participation,

value development,

skill building,

interaction with other troops at the same and at different age levels,

exploration of roles and potentials of women,

understanding and appreciation of several cultures,

active participation in the community.

18 There should be a balance of activities from all program areas, with special attention to the Promise and Law and to what lies ahead in Girl Scouting.

19 Girls and their leaders/advisers should work as partners in planning activities. This partnership increases girl participation and responsibility within each group when a simple form of government is used such as:

Brownie Ring,

patrol system,

steering committee,

town meeting.

20 Troop budgeting should give girls an opportunity to learn money management and decide how their money is to be used. Girls may contribute a portion of their troop treasury to organizations or projects they consider worthwhile.

21 Outdoor activities are an important part of the program for each age level. The type of outdoor experiences should be determined by:

needs and interests of girls,

physical and emotional readiness of girls,

experience/skill level of the girls.

Council approval should be obtained when required. For additional guidance see *Safety-Wise* "Checkpoints for Specific Activities" and camping standards 76 through 96.

22 Recognized health and safety procedures, as outlined in this book, should be followed during all activities.

23 Leaders/advisers, program consultants, or outside instructors working with girls should have the skills and preparation suitable for the level of difficulty of the activity.

24 Service activities or projects should be experienced by all girls. Such activities or projects should be based on the interests of the girls and the needs of the community. Councils should help girls and leaders to identify community needs, locate resources, and plan service projects that are appropriate to the ages and abilities of the girls and follow recognized health and safety procedures. Service incorporates valuable learning experiences in which competition and reward should be neither stimuli nor ends. It is inappropriate to provide awards solely for hours of service, because service is inherent in the Promise and Law.

25 Participation in community events, such as parades, festivals, etc., should be based on needs, interests, and readiness of the girls and should be in line with the "Community Participation" checkpoints in *Safety-Wise.*

26 Troop plans should include ceremonies such as:

investiture for new members to make the Promise and receive their pins,

rededication for girls continuing in the program,

fly-up and bridging/linking for girls moving to the next level of Girl Scouting.

27 Leaders/advisers should work in partnership with girls to decide when requirements for recognitions, such as challenges or badges, have been completed. Decisions should be based upon:

evaluation of performance in relation to abilities and goals,

outline of the recognition in the appropriate publication,

recommendation of program consultant(s) with regard to technical competence.

Parental Permissions

28 Leaders/advisers and girls are responsible for informing parents or guardians of the purpose of Girl Scouting; of the date, time, and place of meetings; and of the type of activities included in troop plans.

29 Leaders/advisers are responsible for informing parents and discussing with them activities involving risk or controversy before the troop makes its activity plans.

30 Leaders/advisers should obtain written parental consent for every girl wishing to participate in an activity that is held at a different place and time from the regularly scheduled meeting, and/or involves unusual risk.

Permission forms used should be developed with council guidance (see "Sample Forms" in *Safety-Wise*).

Transportation

31 All vehicles should be properly licensed and inspected for safety according to state statute or local ordinances.

32 All vehicles should be adequately insured. Drivers should be adults with a valid driving license.

33 Public service carriers/common carriers (i.e., trains and buses) should be used whenever possible.

34 Vehicles should be used for their intended purpose. Vehicles designated primarily to transport equipment and supplies, to serve as recreational homes, or to haul or tow other vehicles should not be used to transport passengers. Exception: hauled vehicles in good condition may be used for hayrides on roads where such vehicles are permitted.

35 Vehicles should not be overcrowded. There should be adequate space for luggage and equipment as well as a seat for each person in the part of the vehicle designated to carry passengers.

36 Adequate adult supervision should be provided (see program standard 3). When a vehicle other than a passsenger car is used, one or more adults other than the driver should be responsible for the group.

37 All passengers should be considerate of the driver and observe safe conduct rules. Precautions should be taken to avoid excessive fatigue for drivers and passengers.

38 All vehicles should be equipped with a first aid kit and any federal- or state-required safety equipment (e.g., spare tire, flares, fire extinguishers, personal flotation devices).

39 All passengers should be informed in advance about accident and emergency procedures.

Uniforms

(Girl Scouting is a uniformed movement as reaffirmed by the National Council in 1969.)

40 Girl and adult members are entitled to wear the Girl Scout uniform. It is suitable at all Girl Scout functions and should be worn appropriately.

41 Members who do not own uniforms should wear the Girl Scout pin. Uniforms are not required for members to participate in Girl Scout activities.

42 The official uniform is particularly appropriate to identify traveling troops and groups or individuals representing the organization.

General Standards for All Troop Money-Earning and Council Product Sales Projects

43 Adults should assume the responsibility for raising the funds to support the Girl Scout council.

44 Troops should be financed primarily by dues from their members. Supplementary troop money earning should be undertaken only when the girls identify and justify the need for such funds.

45 Each girl's and troop's participation should be voluntary.

46 Permission of each girl's parents or guardians should be obtained in writing before she participates in money-earning projects.

47 Girls should understand why the money is needed and learn correct business procedures.

48 Participation should be limited to those girls who are old enough to be businesslike in manner and handle money accurately. Brownies should earn money only through group projects, rather than sales by individuals.

49 Girls and adults should plan and carry out all money-earning projects together.

50 Money-earning projects should be suitable to the ages and abilities of the girls and be positive learning experiences.

51 Girls should be able to earn money in ways that will make them proud of their efforts without promoting undesirable competition. Because the opportunities for success vary greatly it is inappropriate to provide awards for money earning.

52 Local ordinances related to involvement of children in money-earning projects should be observed.

53 Girls should work in pairs, wearing the Girl Scout uniform or pins for identification.

54 When Brownies, Juniors, and/or Cadettes operate booths in stores or public places, an adult should be present at all times.

55 Girls should participate in money-earning projects only during daylight hours, unless accompanied by an adult.

56 Girls should engage in money-earning projects only in neighborhoods that are safe and familiar to them.

57 Parents or other adults should know a girl's whereabouts when she is engaged in money-earning projects.

58 Girls should be familiar with guidelines for personal protection (e.g., do not enter the home of a stranger, know whom to get in touch with in an emergency).

59 Girls should know and use safe pedestrian practices, especially when crossing at busy intersections.

60 Money for products sold should be collected when the product is delivered.

61 Participation of girls and troops in money earning should be limited to projects that do not involve a direct solicitation for cash.

62 Girl Scouts should not take part in actual fund raising for other organizations. Participation of Girl Scouts with appropriate service organizations should be limited to service projects.

63 Council fund-raising efforts, such as United Way and Sustaining Membership Enrollment, should not involve individual girls or troops in any type of direct solicitation for funds.

(See also the following "Troop Money Earning" and "Council Product Sales" sections.)

Troop Money Earning

64 Troop leaders should obtain written permission from their council before starting a troop money-earning project.

65 A troop should not initiate more than one troop money-earning project a year, except in circumstances when funds are needed for special projects.

66 A troop money-earning project should be part of the regular ongoing troop activities and should be suitable for the ages and abilities of the girls.

67 Juniors, Cadettes, and Seniors should be encouraged to earn money through troop projects.

68 The troop should submit a complete report on the troop money-earning project, including evaluation, to the council.

(See also "General Standards for All Troop Money-Earning and Council Product Sales Projects" section.)

Council Product Sales

69 Girls and troops should be involved in no more than two council product sales each year.

70 Leaders/advisers and troop committee members should be involved in the council plans for use of girls in council product sales.

71 A percentage of money earned through product sales should be allocated to the troops, and the exact arrangements should be worked out and interpreted to the leaders in advance.

(See also "General Standards for All Troop Money-Earning and Council Product Sales Projects" section.)

Life-Saving Awards

72 Life-saving awards should be given only to girls. Girls are to have performed heroic acts beyond the degree of maturity and training to be expected at their age.

The Bronze Cross is given for saving life or attempting to save life with extraordinary risk to the candidate's own life.

Honorable Mention is given for saving life or attempting to save life without great risk to the candidate's own life.

Some form of recognition determined by the council may be given for acts of heroism that do not qualify the candidate for either the Bronze Cross or Honorable Mention.

73 Life-saving awards should be given for saving or attempting to save human life only.

74 No life-saving awards should be given to a person who has caused or contributed to the circumstances necessitating the rescue.

75 Awards should only be given to girls who are registered Girl Scouts at the time of the rescue.

Index